Free Enterprise, *Fair* Employment

Books *by* Elliott Jaques

Free Enterprise, *Fair* Employment

Elliott Jaques

Crane Russak · *New York*
Heinemann · *London*

Free Enterprise, Fair Employment

Published in the United States by

Crane, Russak & Company, Inc.
3 East 44th Street
New York, New York 10017
ISBN 0-8448-1417-2

Published in Great Britain by
Heinemann Educational Books
22 Bedford Square
London, WC1B 3HH, England
ISBN 0-435-84420-2

Library of Congress Cataloging in Publication Data

Jacques, Elliott.
    Free enterprise, fair employment.

    1. Wages.   2. Full employment policies.
3. Income distribution.   4. Cost and standard of
living.   I. Title.
HD4906.J35   1982   331.2′1   82-8038
ISBN 0-8448-1417-2   AACR2

Printed in the United States of America

Contents

Contents

To Wilfred Brown

Preface and Acknowledgments

At the time of writing, the democratic industrial nations are in recession, unemployment is rising, and disruptive inflation continues on many fronts. I do not believe that these difficulties are the temporary reflection of just one more economic cycle. We may swing out of them into more prosperous economic times, but we shall not really understand why. We shall therefore be in no better position to avoid a recurrence of this tragedy.

We cannot afford any such recurrences. There is growing despair as well as alienation—as a consequence of the current uncertainties about unemployment, lack of opportunity, and the fears of permanent unemployment on a worldwide scale. These justifiable fears will not just go away. There will be an accumulating distrust of democratic society, unless three prime social conditions are fulfilled: freedom of enterprise; the achievement and maintenance of abundant employment; and the construction of democratic political means for resolving the thorny question of how to achieve a manifestly fair differential distribution of wages and salaries.

Neither classical economic theory nor Marxist theory provides for all three of these fundamental conditions: freedom of enterprise, abundant employment, and fair pay differentials. The failure to deal adequately with them contributes to inflation, to chronic industrial unrest, to the coercive use of power in bargaining, and to widespread despair about the possibility of doing anything constructive about our large-scale bureaucratic employment systems—whether in industry or in commerce, in central or local government, or in social or health services or education.

Thirty-five years of close working contact with these issues in the field—where the problems are—have provided a different background and starting point for tackling the problems. The book outlines this experience, and describes its implications for political economic policy. In writing it, I have moved into academic areas that are normally the preserve of political scientists, economists, and moral philosophers. These are not the times, however, to be too sensitive about such intrusions. I have done so because I believe that a serious alternative to both classical economic theory and socialist theory is possible. This alternative is not a middle-of-the-road compromise but a true alternative, one directed toward the particular circumstances of fully industrialized democratic nations.

The book is the result of close collaboration with Wilfred Brown. It is in this special sense that he shares in any constructive ideas that the book might contain.

The Monument Trust financed my research into employment policies, which led to the idea of the book. I have also had helpful discussions with Sir Roderick Carnegie, Alan Bacon, Rupert Pennant-Rea, and William Helme.

Much of the writing was done in the Center for the Humanities at Wesleyan University in Middletown, Connecticut, where I had the honor to be a Senior Fellow during 1980. I am grateful to Richard Stammelman and his staff for their help.

Miss Rhoda Fowler has taken the manuscript through all the stages of typing and editing and proofreading.

Summary

1.   The most important social and political fact of the twentieth century is that the advanced industrial nations have been transformed into employment societies. Prior to full-scale industrialization, the vast majority of people worked as farmers, traders, craftsmen, or as migrant or limited-term contract labor. With full-scale industrialization, 80 to 90 percent of the working population work as full-time employees on open-ended employment contract.

2.   The dilemma of modern political economy within each nation in the Western industrial world is how to achieve and sustain the following conditions within the constraints of an employment society:

- a strong pluralist political democracy;
- a sound and stable economy free from uncontrolled inflation;
- sufficient opportunity for freedom of enterprise and freedom of consumer choice;
- continuity of employment for the 80 to 90 percent of the working population who are employees;
- a fair distribution of wages and salaries and of socioeconomic status for all those employees.

3.   These conditions have not so far been achieved securely and reliably in the long term. Keynesian demand-pull management appears to be good at generating jobs—but also inflation. Monetarism appears to be good at curbing inflation—but also employment. Mixed economies carry the evils of both and introduce creeping state corporatism as well. No economic policies effectively address the problem of fair wage and salary distribution.

Wage and Salary Leapfrogging (Chapters 1 and 2)
4.   The main difficulty lies not so much in how to deal with the general level of wages and salaries; it lies in the inability to cope at all satisfactorily with the problem of what the differential distribution of wages and salaries—the relativities—ought to be. The assumption that wage and salary differentials can be fixed by the forces of supply and demand on a labor market is inordinately disruptive.

5.   The prime source of wage- and salary-push inflation is the inequity felt in regard to differentials. When one group changes its position in the pecking order, other related groups seek to redress the balance or even to move relatively higher. A continuous process of leapfrogging results; it is stopped in the short term by pay freezes, and subsides in periods of severe unemployment.

6.   Aside from prolonged unemployment, there are three common methods of counteracting wage and salary inflation. One is the short-term pay freeze. The second is productivity bargaining. The third is the establishment of some kind of evaluation system for fixing fair differentials. Pay freezes eventually explode. Productivity bargaining is a euphemism for the buying out of restrictive practices. And job evaluation systems are built up on a false baseline.

The Employment Society: Facts and Fallacies (Chapter 2)
7.   The solution of these problems requires first the recognition of the twentieth-century phenomenon of the coming into existence of the employment society.

8.   It is the employment society which brings with it the turbulent issues of availability of full employment, and of differentials in pay throughout the vast population of employees.

9.   There is a widely held belief—the so-called "lump of labor fallacy"—that the total number of jobs (the lump of labor) is decreasing because of the increasing efficiency of production technology. This belief is false. Any nation can have as much employment as it needs or wishes to have.

10.   A second important fallacy is that wage and salary levels of employees in an employment society can be determined, and fairly, by the market forces of supply and demand. That fallacy is treated at length in the chapters on differential pay and the differential concertina.

Competitive Free Enterprise (Chapter 3)
11.   The valuation of goods and services in terms of an actual purchase price is established by consumer preference; and it is readily established in a competitive market in which there is freedom for entrepreneurs to provide what they judge consumers want, and freedom for consumers to choose what they prefer at a price they are willing to pay.

12.   There are some activities which are the duty and the prerogative of sovereign government and which cannot be left to free competitive enterprise. These sovereign activities include: control of the national

boundary—international relations, defense, immigration, trade and tariffs; and internal controls—institutions of government, taxation, and of the criminal law.

13. In addition, there may be need for government to maintain buffer stocks of public works to provide gap-filling employment to flatten out periods of potential unemployment. It may also be necessary for government to provide some aggregated health, education, and welfare services to ensure an adequate baseline; such services should have to compete with privately provided services.

14. Apart from such governmental activities, all goods and services should be provided on a competitive disaggregated basis. Aggregated centralized governmental services leave it to committees and other statutory bodies to determine what people want without their being given sufficient choice, and without challenge from competing producers to provide alternative choices.

15. There are two types of private entrepreneur: corporate private entrepreneurs; and self-employed private entrepreneurs.

16. Corporate private entrepreneurs are the shareholders and directors of limited liability companies. They earn dividends on their investments and on the possible increases in the value of their shares; and stand to lose on the value of their investment and through getting too small a dividend (or no dividend at all) to pay for the use of their capital. It is important to note that the senior executives of these companies are employees and not private entrepreneurs, and as such receive salaries; those who are also shareholders and directors receive dividends and directors' fees, if any, in addition to salary.

17. Self-employed entrepreneurs include owners of businesses, professionals such as doctors, lawyers, and architects in private practice, and professional artists and athletes. They charge what they wish for their goods and services. Their income derives from their earnings (profits), if any, from the sale of their goods and services. They risk having no income, or suffering losses and going bankrupt, if their earnings are not greater than their expenses.

18. There is a vast difference between the risk earnings of self-employed entrepreneurs and the wages and salaries of people in employment. The entrepreneurs compete for their earnings in an open market, and work simultaneously for a number of different clients or customers. They earn what they can; that is to say, they earn what the market will bear in relation to the particular goods and services they offer.

19.   There is no such thing as fair pay or fair differentials or relativities for entrepreneurs. Entrepreneurs cannot complain that clients or customers are being unfair because some other entrepreneurs are being paid higher prices or fees. Nor can they organize into collectives and threaten to strike so as to shut down their clients' enterprises in order to leapfrog over the prices and fees of other entrepreneurial collectives: that would be restraint of trade. The earnings of the self-employed are thus not to be compared with wage and salary earnings. Entrepreneurial earnings must be left free from restraint to range as high or as low as the vicissitudes of their utility in the market may dictate. They must not be included in any incomes policy.

20.   For entrepreneurs to be able to employ people to further the objects and profitability of the enterprise is a social privilege. It must be no part of free enterprise to profit from paying less than fair wage and salary levels, or from breaking differential equilibrium by paying more. To employ is a social entitlement—to be paid for at the going equitable rate.

21.   For free enterprise to survive, or indeed to be worth safeguarding, the employed population must be assured of steady abundant employment and an equitable differential pay structure. How these can be achieved is the subject of the following sections.

Abundant Employment (Chapter 4)

22.   It will be argued that to be able to exercise our competence to the full in the real world of economically valued work is absolutely essential to the mental health and well-being of human beings.

23.   I believe that no nation has the right to industrialize and become an employment society, if it is to be a reasonably good society, without providing abundant employment for its citizens as a constitutional right. Abundant employment means available employment for those who seek it, at a level consistent with their level of capability.

24.   The consequences of unemployment are socially disastrous. In addition to the fact that the unemployed are demoralized and destitute, those who remain in employment become increasingly underemployed and frustrated because nearly everyone becomes frozen in their existing jobs. The most profound anxieties are stirred throughout society by the forced confrontation with the fact that there are no guarantees that unemployment will ever disappear and no knowing where it will strike next and whom it will strike down.

25.   No nation can be better off for having unemployment. It can only be impoverished. The only possible reason, other than gross political

ineptitude, for having unemployment is to slow down the rate of increase of wages and salaries in order to combat inflation. It is a main theme of the book to show how wage and salary levels can be so arranged as to allow unimpeded abundant employment without its contributing to inflation.

26. The primary sources of abundant employment lie in a buoyant free enterprise and the jobs provided by the sovereign government services.

27. Sufficient venture capital must be available on the money market, supplemented when necessary by government investment resources, to support all reasonable and marginally reasonable entrepreneurial developments. Government support for investment may be necessary to smooth out periods of unavailability of capital and to contribute to the support of high-risk ventures, whether large-scale or small-scale, which might contribute significantly to the national economy.

28. If unemployment should threaten despite increased investment, that is the moment for the introduction of governmental demand—pull measures. There is a need for a buffer stock of central and local government projects which can be carried out on a short-term limited contract basis and used to absorb unemployment. The rates of pay would be those obtaining for equivalent levels of work in open-ended employment.

29. A nation must pay as it goes for eliminating unemployment by its mode of distribution of wages and salaries. Those who are in employment must either stay where they are in pay level or even come down slightly, to produce such redistribution of wages and salaries as may be necessary in connection with the financing of short-term employment opportunities. How this redistribution can be achieved without increasing government borrowing is discussed under the topic of the differential concertina. This marginal redistribution of wages and salaries makes no one actually worse off; but it does substitute some aggregated government services for previously disaggregated services allowing individual freedom of choice.

30. One consequence that it is often thought might follow from abundant employment is that labor mobility might freeze up. In fact there is little evidence that many people move solely for money. The main reason people move is to seek better career opportunities or opportunity for work of particular interest which is not available where they are. Where shortage of housing is an immobilizing factor, the provision of adequate housing is a method par excellence of sustaining decent levels of employment.

31. The main policy must be to bring work to where unemployment

might develop, and for government to provide development area advantages. A subsidiary policy, to encourage labor mobility, must be to allow firms in development areas such as mining and other out-of-the-way natural resource regions, to give substantial special payments to attract those people who can and will move for money; such payments should be made as identifiable special increments and not built into the differential wage and salary structure.

32.   Those who become unemployed should continue to be paid their previous level of pay for a specified period of time during which to seek alternative employment. Under conditions of abundant employment, alternative work should be available, so that involuntary unemployment would be only a temporary state. Those who choose to remain unemployed in an abundant employment society should be entitled to subsistence-level support.

Wage and Salary Levels (Chapter 5)
33.   Wages and salaries are paid as part of the contract of employment.

34.   Employment roles are structured in hierarchical management systems, often known as bureaucracies—in industry, commerce, and public and social services. The payment level (optimally in terms of a pay bracket) should be fixed for each role rather than for the incumbent of the role. If a given person's competence is above that called for in the role, he should be upgraded or promoted to a higher-level role if the opportunity exists, or should transfer to another department or enterprise.

35.   There is thus a structure of higher and lower and equal pay levels related to higher, lower, and equal levels of work. That is the so-called structure of differentials. Employees generally feel that the payment level in any role should be the same as the payment level in other roles at an equivalent work level. A fair wage or salary is a wage or salary that conforms to this differential pattern.

36.   Cross-comparisons can be made between equivalent roles in different enterprises and in different occupational groups.

37.   The structure of wage and salary levels will be seen to be totally different from that of the earnings of self-employed private entrepreneurs. The former is fixed in a hierarchical structure determined by the hierarchical structure of roles in employment systems. The latter is determined by the prices and fees set by individual entrepreneurs in terms of their judgment of what the market will bear for their goods and services. The earnings of self-employed entrepreneurs cannot be contained within the same policies as the wages and salaries of employees.

38.   The differential distribution of wages and salaries may be knocked askew by the forces of supply and demand and by the coercive power of collective bargaining groups; the basic pattern of the distribution of wage and salary levels, however, is not determined by supply and demand. To the extent that market forces and the coercive power of the big battalions distort the fair differential pay pattern related to differential levels of work, this distortion will stimulate resentment, envy and greed, and inflationary leapfrogging.

Equitable Differential Pay (Chapters 6 and 7)

39.   The power of people's feelings of fairness and justice with respect to wages and salaries in employment work is demonstrable in a series of findings from research. The studies have been carried out over the past 30 years in industry, in commerce, in civil service departments, in local government, in social services and health and education: and at all levels from shop and office floor to chief executive officers, and in all occupations.

40.   The first finding is that the level of work in any employment role (but not, it is emphasized, in the roles of self-employed entrepreneurs) can be objectively measured by discovering the tasks or assignments with the longest targeted completion times which a manager assigns into the role of a subordinate. This objective measure is termed the time-span of discretion in the role.

41.   The second finding is that the time-span of the work in a person's role correlates uniquely with that person's judgment of what would be fair pay for the work: people at the same time-span state the same level of felt-fair pay, regardless of actual pay, regardless of occupation, regardless of age, regardless of dirt, danger or discomfort, and regardless of any of the other factors commonly taken into account in job evaluation schemes.

42.   The close relationship between time-span and felt-fair pay has been found in more than twenty different nations. The data run from time-spans of under one day to time-spans of over 20 years, with felt-fair pay levels (in mid-1980) of, for example, $10,000 to over $400,000 in the United States, £3,500 to over £50,000 in the United Kingdom, and $10,000 to over $250,000 in Canada.

43.   The third finding is that employing hierarchies have a systematic requisite underlying structure that is revealed by time-span measurement. They function most effectively and with what feels to people like the proper number of levels of organization, when the following pattern of work-strata is arranged:

Str-VII   Corporate Group Directors

—— 20 Y ————————————————————————————

Str-VI   Corporate Divisional Directors

—— 10Y ————————————————————————————

Str-V   Managing Directors and Top Specialists

—— 5Y ————————————————————————————

Str-IV   General Managers and Chief Specialists

—— 2 Y ————————————————————————————

Str-III   Departmental Managers and Specialist Principals

—— 1 Y ————————————————————————————

Str-II   First-line Managing, Professional and Technical

—— 3 M ————————————————————————————

Str-I   Shop and Office Floor

—— 1 D ————————————————————————————

44.   Each of these work-strata can be divided into grades for purposes of career progression of individuals within their work-strata.

The Differential Concertina (Chapter 8)
45.   These work-strata and grades can be used to state a common differential wage and salary structure for the employee sector of a whole nation by the following procedure.

46.   The national government reviews the economic position each year, and in the light of this' review decides:
   (a)   the general level of wages and salaries the nation can afford to pay itself (in effect, the total wage and salary bill);
   (b)   the differential distribution of those wages and salaries, which it considers to be fair and just.

47.   These decisions are implemented by attaching specific wage and salary figures to the boundaries of each work-stratum and grade. These figures become the wage and salary brackets to be paid to employees. Each employee's role is allocated to a work-stratum and grade by time-span measurement, and attracts the appropriate pay bracket for the role. Everyone employed at the same work-stratum and grade is paid within the same bracket.

48.   This differential pay structure is a unified system which moves

and changes as one total system. It is like a concertina which can be raised or lowered and contracted or expanded ad lib (see diagram on page 91). If a more egalitarian distribution of wages and salaries is desired, the concertina is contracted—either by raising the bottom or by lowering the top, or by both. A wider range of pay levels can be achieved by doing the opposite and expanding the whole system.

49.   So long as the pay relativities are felt by employees to be spread to a just and fair extent, then the general level of pay attaching to the grades can be raised or lowered depending upon economic circumstances, while retaining intact the differential spread and thus everyone's sense of being differentially fairly treated. Everyone gains or loses together. Equity is achieved, and can be seen by the explicit and public differential structure to have been achieved.

50.   Under these conditions of manifestly equitable distribution of wage and salary relativities, it is possible to have continuously abundant employment without stimulating wage- and salary-push inflation. It is possible for any individual employee to get a differential increase relative to others, but only by being upgraded or promoted to a higher level of work.

51.   Establishment of the equitable differential pay structure throughout the employment sector would require substantially fewer specialists than are now employed in most industrial countries on the many and complex job evaluation procedures currently used in industry and commerce and the public services. Attempted abuses by colluding employers and employees can readily be controlled.

Some Features of the Free Enterprise, Fair Employment Society (Chapters 9, 10, and 11)

52.   The mechanism of the differential concertina makes it possible for wage and salary levels to be equitably arranged, and abundant employment maintained, regardless of the economic circumstances of a nation.

53.   It would no longer be necessary to use unemployment to control wage and salary leapfrogging. Full employment and pay differentials having been achieved as political objectives, the problem of regulating the economy would have been substantially simplified.

54.   Political freedom, including free enterprise, would have been strengthened because of the surge in national morale attendant upon securing abundant employment and of the ensuring of fair wages and salaries regardless of the employer.

55.   Abundant employment and equitable pay are the best guarantors of

equal employment opportunity. They would function best where there was adequate opportunity for participation of employees in policy-making in their employing enterprises; and where each generation was expected to make its own way without excessive support for some individuals through inheritance.

56.   Finally, each nation would have to make up its mind about what it considered to be a fair and reasonable workweek. To do this, both the desired standard of living and the nation's assumptions about the psychological need for work would have to be taken into account.

PART ONE
INTRODUCTION

CHAPTER 1

Political Objectives and Economic Regulators in Employment Societies

One of the most important social, political, and economic facts of the twentieth century has been the steady transformation of industrial nations into employment societies. By an employment society I mean a society in which the majority of those who work for a living do so by getting a job on open-ended contract for a wage or salary in a hierarchical employment system. This proportion may reach 80 to 90 percent in advanced employment societies such as Britain and the United States. The existence of the employment society has profound implications for political economic theory and practice, especially in connection with: national policies on employment; wage and salary levels and differentials; political freedom including freedom of enterprise; and the control of inflation and the achievement of a sound economy.

It is my object in this book to analyze some of these implications. In so doing I shall derive what I believe to be the conditions necessary to enable freedom of enterprise and fair and equitable employment to sustain and to nurture each other. It is not, however, part of my object to tackle the complex macroeconomic problems of control of inflation and of the economy. What I shall do is to show how the problems of establishing sound macroeconomic policies may be eased, once the issues of full employment and equitable pay differentials are separated out from the rest and dealt with as political objectives to be achieved in their own right and not used as economic regulators.

The Employment Society

The employment society is a new phenomenon. It is a feature only of advanced industrial nations. Where there is less than full industrialization very few people—perhaps 5 to 10 percent of the working population—are employed on open-ended employment contract in hierarchical employment systems: limited largely to those employed in civil administration, church administration, and the armed services. The vast majority of the working population are otherwise engaged: first, self-employed as farmers, shopkeepers, businessmen, professionals, traders, or craftsmen; and second, employed as migrant or limited-contract labor, or as domestic servants living with the family which engaged them.

The open-ended employment contract first began to be used in industry and then in commerce in Britain in the second half of the nineteenth century. It is a contract in which an employer takes on an employee without setting a termination date. The contract continues until there is a specific act of termination by either party—through dismissal or resignation.

Two main characteristics of being employed on open-ended contract in an employment hierarchy may be briefly outlined (they will be elaborated in Chapter 4). The first is that the taking up of employment constitutes a career for the individual. Full employment opportunities become essential elements in society, not simply in terms of having available work, but in terms of having reasonable security of tenure and opportunity to progress. This type of contract thus leads to very different conditions of employment from those which obtained for migrant labor or for people on fixed-term contract in industry, most of whom were employed by the day—that is to say, they had no security other than day-by-day employment.

The second characteristic is that once large numbers of people gain continuing employment in the hierarchical employment systems which are a feature of industrialized employment societies, they will inevitably make comparisons among themselves of how much they earn, whether as a wage or as a salary. Differentials in wages and salaries become a major issue in society—an issue which grows in importance as the number of people in employment increases. It is not surprising, then, that in employment societies these familiar political aspirations come to the fore: equality of opportunity for everyone in employment and in career; fairness and justice in pay differentials, and collective action to secure them; safeguards against unfair dismissal; proper recognition of service reflected in redundancy (severance) payments; security of economic status in periods of unemployment.

It is these questions that have become entangled with the macroeconomic problems of control of the economy and of inflation. Pressures to sustain fair differentials cause pay leapfrogging; pay leapfrogging causes a self-perpetuating inflationary force, especially in times of full employment; full employment thereby becomes an economic threat rather than a social and political benefit; both unemployment and undifferentiated pay freezes come to be used as instruments of economic regulation; such crude regulators, however, inevitably become politically unacceptable: and in the end, social and political cohesion and morale are undermined, and other macroeconomic measures are weakened, because of the way they are intertwined with the disruptive social forces unleashed by unemployment and by inequitable differential distribution of earnings.

I shall begin my analysis, therefore, by separating out the issues of free enterprise, full employment, and pay differentials, from the host of macroeconomic processes connected with the regulation of a sound economy.

Employment, Economic Equity, and Freedom

There are three paramount needs of people in employment societies which must not only be satisfied but whose satisfaction must be guaranteed if the dignity, the self-respect, and in the deepest sense the sanity of the individual are to be protected and preserved. Those needs are for full employment, fair pay relativities, and political freedom including freedom of enterprise. I emphasize that I am referring to employment societies.

Full employment is necessary both to eliminate the poverty and social deprivation of the unemployed and to give us the opportunity to find work that challenges our capabilities to the full and lets us experience our aptitudes, our realism, our judgment, our competence, our interests, and our ability to work with others, or to exercise leadership and authority. It gives us confidence through economic self-sufficiency and through the self-knowledge we gain and continually renew as we mature and develop new competencies.

Fair pay differentials (and note that I am referring to the *differential* distribution of pay levels, and not the absolute pay levels) allow people to feel part of a cohesive and just society which values its citizens and recognizes their worth, and gives decent relative social and economic status to everyone. Under these conditions everyone's self-esteem is realistically matched against the esteem accorded them by others, and in hard economic terms. It is in these circumstances that one's sense both of reality and of sanity are strengthened.

Political freedom includes the assurance that regardless of race, color, creed, or sex, all citizens shall be equal as citizens and shall share equality of opportunity, including the opportunity to compete to provide the goods and services which will satisfy the needs of others. The consequent free and confident social and political relationships are essential for anyone to be able to feel whole as a person.

These needs are more important than the particular standard of living which people might enjoy. It is possible to tolerate a lowered standard of living in times of national adversity if we know that the consequent suffering is being fairly distributed and encountered by all: in such circumstances national morale and cohesion may be strengthened so that a people may work more cooperatively to overcome the adversity.

I do not believe that the democratic industrial nations have any economic policies or practices which can give manifest assurance that the satisfaction of these fundamental human needs can be secured not just in the short or middle term but in the long term. Full employment which gives to everyone (rather than to an elite) the continuing opportunity for the dignity and self-respect of genuine achievement is assured nowhere as a matter of nationally fixed policy, not even in Japan. Nor are there any specified measures for arranging differential pay in such a manner that employees can both see and feel that justice has been done and a fair and equitable distribution has been achieved. The chronic presence of unemployment and of unfair differential pay is leading increasingly to social alienation, despair, and resentment. Accumulating feelings of being rejected by one's society are a long-term consequence—and I share the not uncommon pessimism about the possibility of safeguarding democracy in industrial societies under these conditions.

The problem of dealing with inflation in the Western democratic nations has further weakened the already tenuous links between economics and economic policies on the one hand and, on the other hand, the life, the humanity, and the emotional stresses of the people whom those policies are meant to serve. The reason lies in the difficulty of gripping in one single controlling context a complex of seemingly contradictory forces and objectives associated with getting inflation under control and keeping it there: to keep up the standard of living and economic growth; to protect democratic freedom and enterprise, and avoid sinking into the pit of totalitarian state corporatism; to maintain free trade between nations; to create the conditions for having full employment; and the hope that an equitable distribution of incomes and of socioeconomic status will somehow be arranged by the forces of supply and demand in the labor market.

None of the prescribed economic policies copes with all the facets of the problem. Keynesian demand—pull procedures can overcome unemployment, but not without pushing the distribution of pay toward increasing differential disequilibrium and thereby giving rise to cost—push inflationary forces. By contrast, the procedures associated with the monetarists appear to be accompanied by excessive and wasteful unemployment. Milton Friedman's own prescription for obviating this effect by introducing gradual change has not been tested; but in any case it is unlikely to help because it contains no means of dealing with wage and salary differentials and leapfrogging, other than by relying on market forces—and I shall establish in the next chapter why that solution is unlikely to work. The supply-side approach suffers from the same shortcoming.

The liberal and social democratic middle-of-the-road mixed economy proponents do strive after full employment, but run into these same troubles. Nationalization and centralized governmental provision of high levels of social and welfare services, combined with free enterprise, can give full employment and can even sometimes lead to economic successes, in the short and middle terms of two to ten years (as may demand-side and supply-side policies). They can do so particularly in the early stages of periods of reflation, or in circumstances where a nation which has lagged behind economically is beginning to catch up, so that everyone is experiencing the satisfactions of an expanding economy. But in the longer term, in the absence of policies for sustaining equitable pay differentials, these differentials get out of line, generating leapfrogging inflation which ends up in excessive government spending and money supply and a tendency for the nation to live beyond its means. Price controls which interfere with free enterprise, and freezes on wage and salary levels which also rigidify differentials, must then be introduced. That is when the real trouble starts. Either there is a sharp increase in industrial unrest, or malignant chronic inflation sets in, or both.

By contrast, state corporatism based upon Marxist political economy is capable of maintaining employment, but only by means of oppressive and economically inefficient state control and military-backed suppression of political freedom and freedom of enterprise which hold down the standard of living. State corporatism (like nationalization) merely moves the scene of negotiations about differential pay to the government on behalf of the people. And there is no evidence that the people, through their government, are any more capable of equitable treatment of the people they employ than are private employers. In many respects they are worse. Like classical political economy, Marxist theory with its unimplementable dictum of ". . . to each according to his needs" has in reality no means other than a supply-and-demand theory for determining the distribution of relative socioeconomic status by means of wage and salary income differentials.

In short, it would appear that the Achilles heel of current economic nostrums is their inability, at least in the long term, to handle both the problems of full employment and of wage and salary differentials. Keynes recognized that demand – pull measures lead to inflation and eventual unemployment, but had no proposals for doing anything about it. The supply-siders and the monetarists mostly seek to deny that any special measures have to be taken with respect to wage levels and differentials, preferring to leave them to be controlled by market forces and unemployment (or they overlook the problem of differentials altogether); hence their policies lead to a tendency for wage- and salary-push inflation to increase as unemployment begins to fall. And unfortunately those economists who would seek to combine incomes policies with either demand-side or supply-side measures are not sure what to do: they lean toward assisting the operation of the labor market by means of a periodic imposition of price and income freezes, rather than by a deeper consideration of just what a policy of fair wage differentials might entail.

To resolve these difficulties will require more than good intentions. It demands a substantial reorganization of our employment institutions and of the political economic theories on which they are founded. It is no more use having good intentions with bad institutions than it is having good institutions with bad intentions: in the first case good intentions are subverted; in the second case good institutions are abused.

The Confusing of Objectives with Instruments

Every nation longs both for reasonable economic prosperity and for reasonable economic stability. What is accepted as reasonable will vary with circumstances. The steady growth of GNP is not necessarily essential, despite the fact that the Western world has become so attached to that idea. The degree of prosperity already enjoyed, the availability of national resources, the state of the international market, the existing level of productivity, the assumptions about what constitutes an acceptable workweek, will all affect the national view about how satisfactory is the national standard of living.

Moreover, the views about standard of living have now become substantially influenced by desires for stability, as a result of the unsettling experience of worldwide accelerating inflation during the past fifteen years. How to be sufficiently prosperous without the chronic threat of that prosperity's being sucked dry by inflation has become the dominant problem of economic policy in most countries.

The arguments about economic growth and inflation necessarily raise all the questions about what is the best type of political system. The advantages of competitive free enterprise, democratic socialist mixed economies, and nationalization and state corporatism are all persuasively pressed by their proponents. Except for the political repression which accompanies state corporatism, there has been little solid evidence so far that any of the alternative national policies will be politically and economically more satisfactory in the long run than any other.[1]

Interlocked with the problem of inflation is the problem of full employment. During the 1930 depression unemployment was the key issue, and Keynesian economics swept the field. Today, unemployment is treated by many politicians and economists as less important than inflation, because of the repeated experience that full employment fans inflation. Full employment without inflation is one of the most elusive of economic objectives.

Dogging all these issues is the chronic unrest and disaffection arising from the problem of how to distribute income and socioeconomic status in a manner that can be experienced as fair and proper. Continually repeated sequences of coercive power-bargaining over pay and pay differentials is endemic in the absence of any generally acceptable principles of how to settle pay relativities. The argument is pitched in terms of whether some form of incomes policy is needed for the successful implementation of either supply-side or demand-side programs, or whether income levels should not be tampered with but left to the genuinely free play of the labor market. There is little awareness of the fact that pay differentials might be a political distribution problem to be dealt with in a fundamental way in their own right by political means.

These four main objectives—political freedom, full employment, fair differential distribution of wages and salaries, and a reasonable standard of living without internally created inflation—need to be treated as separate and clearly defined objectives, each in its own right. Dealt with as separate objectives, they can be considered in relation to one another; therein lies some hope of understanding how they interact

---

[1] Japan may be the exception to this view, because of a combination of three factors: its consensual *gemeinschaft* culture which pervades its industry and makes for healthy industrial relations and employer-employee cooperation; its tendency toward a systematic organizational structuring (and system of titles) which makes for status security and efficiency in work; and its financing of its businesses by its banking system, which engenders greater responsibility for its businesses than does an open investment market. But even so, as I have mentioned above, I believe that in the long term Japan, as it becomes a fully industrialized employment society, will suffer the same fate as the other industrial nations, unless it develops effective measures for coping with the problems of differential wage and salary distribution, and unless it is able to assure full employment for all, including the lower levels of workers employed in large enterprises.

and how they influence one another. Unfortunately, they tend to be treated together, and admixed with a plethora of other factors connected with the regulation of the economy—factors which must include the question of the total amount (the general level) of wages and salaries as against the differential distribution of that total amount. In the mix-up, full employment and wage and salary equity are lost sight of as prime social and political objectives, and get swept up as instruments to be used along with other instruments of economic regulation to counter inflation.

Thus it is that controls of income levels which also freeze relativities become one component of most of the economic policies and measures geared to the fight against inflation; or else they do not satisfactorily address the problem of relativities at all. In the same vein, full employment becomes a threat rather than a benefit, it carries pay inflation pressures in its wake. Therefore, the level of employment also must be carefully controlled: such control is a euphemism for keeping that level of unemployment which will restrain the leapfrogging wage increases which are driven by the forces of dissatisfaction over pay-differential inequity. Even those who go all out for the absolute primacy of monetary control must rely implicitly upon the unemployment consequences of tight money to hold down this kind of leapfrogging pay inflation, even though they might not wish to admit it.

Seen from the perspective of regulation of the economic system to control inflation, levels of employment and the distribution of wage and salary differentials get thrown in with that great conglomeration of instruments of macroeconomic control whose significance and priority for attention at any given time are the target of so much argument among politicians, economic policy-makers, economists, civil servants, and business and trade union leaders. These macroeconomic factors include, for example: the general level of wages and salaries (as against their differential distribution); the quantity and velocity of circulation of money, stated in terms of whichever of the M1, M2, M3, etc. forms happens to be the most seriously relevant, or perhaps fashionable; the ruling rate of interest set by the central bank or by the banking system; the level of savings and modes of encouraging or discouraging savings; the level of industrial investment, and modes of ensuring a steady flow of venture capital; the scale of total government borrowing, the public spending borrowing rate, and the size of the national debt; the rate of exchange for the currency, and the need for government support to maintain the exchange rate at a level which is optimum for the balance of export trade; the international market prices for various commodities, including key commodities such as oil, foodstuffs, and raw materials; the level of international trade, and the country's own balance of overseas trade; price levels on the home market; the rate of profit being earned by private enterprise; the price of gold; the levels of direct and indirect taxation, the relativities between corporate and personal taxation, and the pattern of graduation of taxation relative to incomes; population demography and levels of pension and social benefits; the skill of the population; the likely impact of new technologies.

The list of significant macroeconomic factors, all of which must be taken into account in economic planning, can easily be extended. It is not necessary to do so for our purposes. The difficulties of foreseeing how changes in any part of this complex economic system will impact upon other parts are notorious. Unexpected consequences continually arise. And there are always unanticipated occurrences—from natural catastrophes to new discoveries, to the sudden emergence of new industrial economies, to new political and economic alliances, to outbreaks of war and of peace—to confound the experts and to confound or negate even the most successful of short-term and middle-term policies and prophecies.

I shall not deal directly with this complex interplay of macroeconomic issues connected with maintaining stable national economies and with the control of inflation. I shall, however, deal with them indirectly by separating out the two most politically explosive forces—full employment, and wage and salary differentials—and treating them separately, within a competitive free enterprise context, as political economic issues which can be dealt with in their own right. By separating out these two issues and dealing with them on their own, I believe that the task of macroeconomic policy-making can be significantly simplified, and for two reasons: first, the disruptive influence of the two most politically sensitive variables will have been removed from the macroeconomic debate; and, second, full employment and equitable pay differentials (as I shall demonstrate) can be achieved once they are dealt with separately as political issues, with the result that a confident public outlook will be created as the foundation for more constructive public argument about the economy.

By contrast with this procedure, if level of employment and wage and salary distribution are manipulated as part of the complex of instruments of macroeconomic control, any emerging economic policy will inevitably be dehumanized. Full employment fulfills a deep human need; everyone simply knows that to use unemployment to try to control inflation is wrong, because no nation can be better off as a result of unemployment, whatever the other economic circumstances. Wage and salary differential distribution is in the same category. I shall demonstrate in Chapter 6 that there exists a fair differential pay structure at any given time and that it can be discovered. There is no reason why this distribution of wage and salary relativities should not be maintained so that the accompanying relativities in socioeconomic status may in turn be fair and just whatever the general economic conditions might be.

Full Employment and Fair Wage and Salary Distribution as Objectives

The significant point is that level of employment and differential patterns of wages and salaries can be dealt with in their own right. They need to be handled as the political and social objectives they are, and not to be reduced to instruments of economic recovery and control. I shall demonstrate that when employment and pay differentials are handled in this way, they make for a fully competitive free enterprise that is most consistent with the ideology of freedom within democratic pluralism, and in particular with a democracy that pays its way as it goes. Fully competitive free enterprise includes freedom of pricing and of profitability, with the protection for consumers and for employees lying precisely in the freedom of competition, the state of full employment, and the arrangement of equitable wage and salary differentials.

The major political objectives, then, which I shall highlight are:

- fully competitive free enterprise, with freedom of consumer choice, the goods and services offered, and their prices, determined by competition, and risk and profits and losses taken by entrepreneurs and investors;
- abundant employment in the sense of work for those who wish to work, available at a level consistent with the capability of the individual;
- equitable differentials in wage and salary levels (which will be shown to be related to level of work carried) not subject to unfair manipulation either by employers or by employees;
- a sound economy with as good a standard of living as the natural resources, technology, capital wealth, and human resources of the nation can provide, and without malignant internally induced inflation.

The first three of these objectives are attainable in their own right, and can be sustained independently of other economic conditions. They do not require complex manipulation of the economic system. The fourth objective is the one which is different: it does require attention to a wide range of economic variables, such as those illustrated in the list above. I shall address the first three objectives; I shall consider the fourth only to the extent necessary to show that the task of deciding macroeconomic policies in a nation may be simplified if the first three objectives are independently assured.

If it is true that free enterprise, abundant employment, and equitable wage and salary distribution are achievable in their own right as political objectives, then it may be self-evident that the complex problems associated with sustaining a sound and stable economy would be greatly simplified. Consumer needs would be catered for as far as the national talent allowed. Price levels would be allowed to take care of themselves. Profitability would be justified by service and by the acceptance of the risk of loss. Wage and salary differential levels would not be subject to the play of coercive power and exploitation.

The net effect would be a nation better able to carry on with the task of continuously adapting to changes in economic circumstances. Thus, for example, inflationary forces arising through increases in the purchase price of raw materials and other imports would have to be sorted out internally and fully considered in the context of the standard of living the nation can afford in the changed circumstances. That is to say, disruptive inflationary forces would not be let loose from inside the nation; they would arise only from outside and could be met by a national sharing of the problem, and by the equitable distribution of suffering or of gain. There would be no need to try to provide an excessive quantity of money or to borrow one's way out of the problem; those needs arise when there is no mechanism for equitable distribution of employment and income, and when those who have try to hang on to what they have at the expense of everyone else.

Wage and Salary Differentials as the Floating Variable
When I say that free enterprise, abundant employment, and equitable wage and salary distribution can be achieved on their own, there is still one problem which must be overcome. It *can* be overcome. It is the problem of eliminating that element of inflation that arises from continuous inflationary movements in wages and salaries and the well-known stickiness downward of payment levels. In view of the wide differences of opinion about the importance to be attached to wage and salary differentials in relation to the control of inflation and the achievement of full employment, I shall turn in the next chapter to a consideration of how these pay levels get settled at present, and the effects of those settlements upon the economy.

CHAPTER 2

Coercive Bargaining and Wage and Salary Differentials

There are at present no satisfactory arrangements for determining either the general level of wages and salaries in a nation or the distribution of wage and salary differentials. Two main types of procedure are used in the democratic industrial nations: free collective bargaining and incomes policies.

Free collective bargaining is to some extent a misnomer. It is certainly free in the sense that the winning of the freedom for workers to organize to take collective action in pursuit of better working conditions was a significant political gain. But that political advance has now been tarnished by the fact that, in practice, the freedom to act collectively grants freedom to the most powerful to wrest advantages for themselves by· coercion, to the disadvantage of the less powerful. This coercive element is created by the fact that free collective bargaining refers to a multiplicity of separate collectives, each pursuing its own particular ends, inevitably, if successful, at the expense of others. It is this fragmented negotiation process, rooted in the exercise of coercive power, that will be discussed in this chapter in connection with the problem of the chronic restlessness over pay differentials which stirs and fuels incessant inflationary pay leapfrogging.

As to the second of the two procedures—incomes policies—these tend to come on the scene as a means of controlling the leapfrog excesses of coercive bargaining. They are mostly limited either to the setting of temporary pay freezes or the fixing of limits to pay increases, or to the use of so-called productivity bargaining. It will not be difficult to show that pay freezes and limitations are crude processes that can hold only for limited periods of time, and that productivity bargaining is a euphemism for the disruptive procedure of buying-out restrictive practices and of paying bonuses to bribe people to do a fair day's work.

In considering collective bargaining and incomes policies, it is useful to keep in mind that despite their shortcomings in practice, they are in a different world politically from the autocratic imposition of pay levels and differentials which, in the absence of sound principles, are the means that corporate socialist states have used for dealing with these problems.

Let us therefore consider these two procedures and their consequences. In order to do so, it is essential first of all to establish a clear and unequivocal distinction between incomes in the sense of the wages and salaries gained by employees, and the profits or losses earned by self-employed entrepreneurs. Collective bargaining is concerned only with fixing wages and salaries and not with self-employed earnings.

Employee Wages and Salaries and Self-Employed Earnings

It is common, in discussions about income levels, to fail to distinguish between on the one hand the earnings of self-employed entrepreneurs such as, for example, film stars, surgeons in private practice, professional athletes, with on the other hand the wages and salaries of those who are in employment, such as skilled workers in factories, nurses in hospitals, and government and other employees.[1] This failure to discriminate sharply between the earnings of the self-employed and the wages and salaries of employees has two very grave consequences.

The first consequence is that the notion that wages and salaries and entrepreneurial earnings are all the same supports the idea that wages and salaries are part of one and the same market mechanism by means of which differentials in self-employed earnings are competitively determined. It will be an important part of my argument to show why it is theoretically unsound and socially and economically disruptive to believe that differentials in wages and salaries between employees can simply be left to be determined by such competitive market mechanisms. Here is a prime case of bad theory supporting the continuation of bad practice.

From these misleading ideas about a labor market, contradictory and equally misleading conclusions are drawn. On the one hand, it is concluded that collective bargaining is a competitive market process like any other market competition; thus, competitive collective bargaining ought (so long as the money supply is adequately controlled) to provide realistic and noninflationary wage and salary levels. On the other hand,

---

[1] Friedman, for example, fails to make this distinction, taking the wages of loggers in the lumber industry and the earnings of Frank Sinatra, Red Adair, and other self-employed stars as equivalent instances of income, all subject to the same market forces. As I shall show in this and succeeding chapters, he thus unnecessarily weakens much of his argument about the market, incentives, and income distribution. M. Friedman and R. Friedman, (1979), *Free to Choose*. New York: Harcourt, Brace, pp. 18–24.

it is concluded that what is needed is to abolish all collective bargaining and to achieve a market process in which individual employees are truly free to bargain for their own individual pay. I shall show that both these contradictory conclusions are untenable, and that they promote unsound policies.

The second consequence is that invidious comparisons are made in negotiation discussions between the very high incomes earned by outstanding stars and professionals and the wages and salaries of employees including those occupying high-level managerial positions. Attempts to introduce incomes policies are then beset by the problem of whether or not such policies should apply to self-employed entrepreneurial earnings. If only wages and salaries are subject to the policy, the trade unions complain that the private profit-makers get off scot free; if the latter are included, then the self-employed entrepreneurs are entitled to complain of a gross interference with private enterprise and initiative.

The fact is, of course, that wages and salaries, and self-employed earned incomes, are very different from each other. The former are based upon open-ended employment contracts, and are ensured so long as the person is in employment. By contrast, the earnings of the self-employed entrepreneur are in no way assured. They will vary with a person's reputation or marketing skill. And the amount of the earnings at any given time may vary from a very high running income to very low levels, or even to zero income or a loss. The risk of profit or loss, earning or no earning, lies with the entrepreneur.

Moreover, it is perfectly legal and proper for employees to organize and to negotiate collectively for common levels of pay. It is improper for self-employed entrepreneurs to do so, for that would constitute a restraint of trade. In the discussion that follows, I shall consider collective bargaining and incomes policies in relation only to the wages and salaries of employed persons. I shall consider in later chapters, as separate questions, the problem of entrepreneurial earnings and the problem of better ways of establishing adequate differentials in wages and salaries.

Coercive Bargaining and Inflationary Pay Leapfrogging
A common fallacy in economics lies in the belief that wage and salary differentials can be satisfactorily contained by the market forces of supply and demand. There is a failure to take into account the intensity of people's feelings about fairness and justice in relativities in wages and salaries. There are no equivalent feelings among entrepreneurs: one self-employed person may envy the success of another, but the issue of differential fairness and justice does not reasonably arise.

It is the instability in the structure of wage and salary differentials which causes what I would term self-generating and self-perpetuating inflation; that is to say, inflation which perpetuates itself as a result of uncontrollable forces from within a given economy. Self-generating inflation in this sense is to be sharply differentiated from inflation caused by external forces such as a worldwide increase in the price of commodities which have to be imported, or fluctuations in currency exchange rates. These externally forced increases affect all nations. They also affect each nation as a whole.

The reason why instability in pay differentials stimulates the malignancy of self-generating inflation is not far to seek. The structure of differential pay is like the surface of a choppy sea. It is never still. Waves keep popping up relative to the rest of the surface, then subside while other parts reach up relatively higher. Underneath the choppy surface there lies the steady groundswell of inflation.

The prime forces which drive this restless choppy motion are not, however, the forces of labor supply and demand. The so-called labor market is not a competitive atomistic market. It does not behave like the market for, say, copper. The prime forces with respect to the price differentials for labor lie in the strivings of people to change their pay position relative to others in terms of their feelings about the fairness of the current differentials or of established precedents. As soon as collective group A gets an increase, then groups B, C, and D and many others feel entitled to an equivalent increase in order to keep their position in the pecking order, or the incomes ladder or the earnings league table, as the hierarchy of differentials is variously called. Each increase thus sets up a chain reaction, regardless of the supply and demand situation.

What does not happen is that as labor scarcity develops in some sectors the pay levels go up in those sectors and retain their differentially high position until the scarcity subsides. Nor do the pay levels decrease either absolutely or differentially as an oversupply of labor develops in certain sectors. They do not even stay still, but may move upward if the differential pay balance is disturbed, unless the economy is deeply depressed and unemployment is high.

Whether or not, therefore, any particular collective group presses for an increase, and adds its quota of energy to the bargaining pressure kettle, is determined not primarily by the market situation, nor by the cost of living, but by the group's sense of whether or not it has been losing out relative to others. These feelings and actions hold even where there is unemployment, as current experience of stagflation with moderate to high unemployment has shown.

This argument is not intended to suggest that market forces have no effect at all. They do have some effect. But not the effect that economic market theory would lead us to expect. Market forces act mainly to disrupt the established pattern of differentials: employers may attempt to drive harder bargains over pay if there is a surplus of labor available; and employees may do the same in times of labor shortages. If they succeed, it will be only for a short time. For the groups of workers or staff who have been left differentially behind will thenceforth continually attempt to surge ahead again and leapfrog themselves back into what they consider their rightful differential position (or even higher, since that gives a margin for negotiation).

So it is, for example, that a local or central government may decide that its teachers are well enough paid because no one is leaving the profession and there are plenty of teachers available, but that its nurses are entitled to an increase because they are leaving and there is a growing shortage. That argument will not convince the teachers if they feel that the differentials were about right. The employer's response to the market will leave the teachers in a state of disaffection; and eventual militant action to "restore the proper differentials" can be anticipated.

Where this inordinately powerful sense of rightful differentials comes from if it does not derive from market forces, will be considered in Chapter 6. But in the absence of any principles for settling the total pattern of differentials, the only alternative is the exercise of coercive power contained in the right of employees to strike, combined with the right of the employer to hold out against the strike. Thus, whether any particular group will succeed in gaining or regaining what it considers to be its rightful place in the economic sun depends upon the coercive power it can muster. The most powerful groups are those which are most cohesively organized and which can do most damage to the nation as a whole; for example by shutting down its electric power, or its air services or its telecommunications.

In short, the pattern of the differential distribution of wage and salary incomes in capitalist and social democratic industrial societies is in large part determined by coercion—the coercion of the big battalions in the bargaining situation. Who the big battalions will be at any given time will be settled by the power situation: it may be certain trade unions, highly organized, in economically successful industries or in nationalized industries, who will be able to bargain themselves on to a relatively high rung on the incomes ladder. Or in times of unemployment everyone, including those who are differentially depressed anyway, may be suppressed by tough-minded employer attitudes or by tough governmental controls.

As a result of this continuous play of the coercive power game, industrial nations are not only prey to self-generating inflation, they are likely to become progressively radicalized. This effect is reduced so long as there is steady economic growth to absorb some of the differential inequities. Thus, for example, no democratic nation can afford to sustain a steady economic state without economic growth, even in circumstances where such a state of equilibrium might be desirable. For differential tensions would build up and send the system into disequilibrium and cost−push inflation.

Finally, it is because of these differential tensions that wages and salaries are almost totally inelastic downward. No group will give up its position relative to others—not even a differentially favorable position. There is no conceivable principle currently extant by means of which it could agree to do so. The only correcting mechanism which people will accept is upward: the overcoming of felt-unfair differentials is a one-way upward road to malignant inflation. As Trevithick notes, Keynes was well aware that the downward inflexibility of pay was due to the near impossibility of breaking the pattern of differentials. The Keynesian economist Hicks has also been clear about the significance of differentials.[2]

Damaging Social Consequences of Coercive Bargaining

The full and damaging consequences of settling pay disputes by coercive power have not been sufficiently recognized or articulated. Apart from the terrible cost in malignant inflation, there is a cost in social despair and alienation, in suspicion and distrust, arising from the deep

---

[2] Trevithick usefully summarizes Keynes's view on this issue: "When discussing the failure of money wages to fall in times of quite massive unemployment, Keynes regarded such downward inflexibility as being the product of highly structured *wage differentials*. Wage bargaining was (and still is) a decentralised process in which a decision by one particular group to accept a cut in its money wage rate will probably not be followed by similar money wage cuts by other groups. Wage cuts are therefore resisted even in the face of considerable unemployment. Workers are apprehensive lest their position in the pecking order of wage differentials be damaged by following what, in simple classical theory, appears to be a rational course of action. Keynes insisted that, in practice, the operation of collective bargaining sets great store by the preservation of a highly stable pattern of wage differentials. The interconnection between differential labour markets is so pronounced that any attempt at altering the structure of differentials will be strongly resisted by the groups whose relative position is threatened. Workers will go to great lengths 'to protect their *relative* real wage' and will resist any move which will disturb this relative wage. It is a well-known fact of the industrial-relations experience of most western economies that wage claims based upon comparability with other groups constitute a large proportion of all wage claims and that, if these claims are successful, they will generate a highly stable pattern of differentials over time." J.A. Trevithick, (1977), *Inflation: A Guide to the Crisis in Economics*. Harmondsworth: Penguin Books Ltd., p. 68.

sense of differential injustice and of coercion (and of there being no constructive way of righting the injustice because the only means at hand is to exercise coercive power against others in return) that has never been calculated. Let us outline these costs and put the account straight.

The first cost is the impact of treating the human capability and creativity of employees as commodities-for-hire whose relative value is to be settled by coercive power. That process has a degrading effect, and any economic or social theory which overlooks or disregards this effect is disqualified from the start. It is human integrity and human dignity which are at stake in coercive collective bargaining.

The second cost is the impact upon the cohesion of society itself of coercive collective bargaining. Collective bargaining, which was a great step toward political freedom in the nineteenth century, has turned into its opposite. The political freedom to organize has been established, and elimination of that freedom is universally recognized as oppression. But because of the coercive manner in which that freedom is now exercised, collective bargaining has paradoxically become oppressive in its turn: freedom requires different outlets.

Collective bargaining procedures, then, favor coercive power. A society which has recourse to these procedures is openly sanctioning coercion. Those who come out on top encounter a conflict of feelings: on the one hand, they feel justified in their actions, for the only way to get ahead under collective bargaining is to forget about others and to beat your way as high up as possible—and in any case it is the employer who pays; on the other hand, they feel guilty at heart—unless they deny and destroy those feelings, in which case there are deeper and less conscious feelings of being persecutors and of being liable to persecution in return which will be stirred. Feelings of envy are aroused all round—spiteful envy felt for those who have coerced their way into advantageous positions, and envy felt by these latter for those who have done even better. Envy feeds greed, and the essence of greed is that it can never be satisfied—at the social level it stirs violence.

I am not here trying to paint a picture of everyone's being consciously envious and greedy and consciously spending all their time worrying about their own and everyone else's relative economic position. But I am saying that these feelings lie festering—sometimes strongly and sometimes vaguely in the background, but festering nonetheless. As such, they are a constant and continual source of malice, steadily poisoning people's attitude toward their society, sometimes only incipiently but sometimes overwhelmingly.

Moreover, these negativistic feelings are socially sanctioned feelings, because the procedures which give rise to them are socially sanctioned. They thereby become the kinds of feelings that sensible and realistic people ought to have. They become part of society's real morality and ethics as against its social teaching; of its morality and ethics as lived and experienced in our real everyday lives as against the morality and ethics of the moral and religious tenets to be found in books. As such they contribute to the stockpile of unresolvable conflict and violence, a stock which does not drain away but builds up through time, like atomic waste, depressing the vitality and the will to maintain a good society and reducing the ability to do so. Justice and freedom are the victims.

Despite these difficulties the untenable system of market-determined wage and salary differentials is, of course, supposed to be economically efficient. The theory is that as given types of commodities become more desirable to the market and the numbers of jobs available in those sectors increase, there will be an increased demand for labor and there will then follow a differential increase in pay, until the required number of new employees has been attracted.

Things do not, however, simply work out in accord with this theory of labor mobility. It does not necessarily happen that labor mobility increases. Rather, to the extent that scarcity of supplies of labor—or indeed any other factor—drives up the rates of pay differentially in one sector compared with others, then a differential instability is introduced with its consequent wage and salary leapfrogging.

Current theory would have it that if only there were a perfect market these inflationary effects would not be harmful, since they would reflect the movement of labor to the most economically important sectors of the economy. It is recognized, however, that the market is not perfect, so therefore other means of controlling the damaging inflationary effects of the imperfections are needed. The first of these means is unemployment itself. It is one of the major tragedies of the Western industrial democracies—one of the prime sources of seemingly justified violence and delinquency—that the retention of a certain amount of unemployment is seen as necessary for the control of wage−push and salary−push inflation. The second means consists of various types of incomes policy, to which I shall now turn.

Inadequacy of Pay Freezes and Productivity Bargains
Other attempts to control malignant wage− and salary−push inflation are directed mainly toward incomes policies. None of these incomes

policies, however, adequately tackles the problem of differentials. They are all concerned with the control of wages and salaries either by putting controlled ceilings on increases or by somehow associating increases with productivity.

The policy of setting controlled ceilings is notoriously troublesome. If there is a general restriction, say a maximum of 6 percent for negotiated increases, then two difficulties arise. First, those who obtained increases of more than 6 percent just before the freeze are differentially better off, and are experienced by others as having had an unfair advantage—to be made up for as soon as the control ceiling is lifted. Second, all negotiations for wage and salary increases tend to level out at an all-round 6 percent; consequently not only is there no leeway for correcting any existing differential inequity, but for some who do not get the full 6 percent the position is worsened. The failure over a period of time to adjust differentials leads to an all-round buildup of frustration.

The other alternative—namely, the associating of wage and salary increases with increases in productivity—is based upon an untenable economic theory and is just as troublesome as wage and salary freezes. The theory is that payment tied, for example, to piecework incentive payment systems or to agreements to increase productivity are noninflationary. The costs of increased pay are supposedly picked up in the value of increased output.

This theory about productivity does hold at the macroeconomic level. That is to say, for a nation to increase its total GNP in real terms entitles everyone within it to an increase in standard of living without that increase stirring malignant inflation. Such increases in GNP usually come from investment in improved methods, better products and services, and better overseas marketing. The whole nation is affected by such upsurges, and the whole nation should share in the gain.

At the microeconomic level, however, the picture is totally different. It is not true that particular individuals or groups within a given economy can differentially be singled out for special productivity payments without those payments being inflationary. The fallacy in the theory as applied at the microeconomic level is the assumption that individual employees can do anything positive beyond the requisite normal conditions of the employment contract to increase their productivity. By the requisite normal conditions of the employment contract is meant: first, that employees will do a reasonable day's work; second, that they will use such initiative and ability as they have to improve their performance by improving their own methods of working; and third, that they will accept new methods of working introduced by management.[3] Any individual improvement in performance ought to be rewarded by individual merit reviews based upon performance appraisal; and extreme competence as shown, for example, in repeated outstanding innovation ought to be rewarded by promotion. If, however, any new methods which are introduced can be shown to lead to increases in the level of work, then the pay level should be adjusted accordingly; if the new methods are not familiar to the employee, then retraining must be provided; and if they could lead to loss of jobs and redundancy, then the conditions of their introduction should be negotiated in advance (as argued in Chapter 10).

Given these requisite normal contractual conditions, the only employees who can individually increase their productivity are those who are not doing a reasonable day's work or are otherwise engaged in restrictive practices. The way they can increase their productivity is by beginning to do a reasonable day's work or by giving up restrictive practices. Productivity deals, therefore, reward those who have not been doing a fair day's work or have been successfully maintaining restrictive practices; those doing a fair day's work without restrictive practices can get no increase.

This situation occurred in Britain between 1965 and 1970. A national incomes policy was established in which no increase in wages or salaries could be negotiated unless it could be shown that the bargaining group would give an increase in productivity equivalent to the increase in pay. There ensued a period of almost five years in which the only people who got increases were those workers who had a restrictive practice to sell. Those groups which did not have any restrictive practices to sell, such as nurses, managers, teachers, got no increases. What happened was a piling up of differential inequities over the years so that the policy began to crumble toward the end of the five-year period. Meanwhile the unions and associations representing such groups as nurses and teachers became intensely militant, and there began the practice of closing hospitals and schools by strikes, a practice which has now become well established. In a similar vein, the managers' trade union, ASTMS, became one of the fastest-growing unions in Britain during the 1970s. I believe that the deep-seated dishonesty inherent in productivity bargaining, however unwitting it may have

---

[3] It is a valid implication from this argument that all work normally leads to a continual increase in productivity. That consequence is inevitable, since it is impossible for human beings in normal circumstances to continue to do a job without learning from experience at least marginally.

been, was a major blow to national cohesion in Britain, and that it left a legacy of mistrust that lasted through the 1970s.

To Each According to His Needs?

If classical economic theory misses the point as far as wage and salary payment and differentials are concerned, is there any chance that perhaps Marxist theory, with its professed concern for workers, might do any better? By Marxist theory in this context, I refer to the elimination of all competitive market mechanisms—both the free competitive market for goods and services and the competitive labor market—because of the hope that ownership of the means of production by the state on behalf of the people can prevent the exploitation of employees by employers.[4] The dropping of the concept of labor market might have been helpful, but unfortunately notions of valuation of labor in terms of supply and demand have been retained, albeit in the setting of governmental control rather than the operation of the marketplace. The dropping of the market valuation of goods and services is simply a big mistake.

The elimination of a free competitive labor market could have been a step forward. However, what could have been a good idea based upon an interesting if unrealistic principle for determining differentials has in fact been thrown away. That principle is Marx's dictum of "from each according to his abilities, to each according to his needs." The difficulty with such a principle is that no one can assess the abilities of individuals, and there is most certainly no way (other than a free competitive market) of assessing relativities in needs.

One consequence of the failure of this impracticable idea has been the widespread application by socialist nations of a watered-down version of supply and demand theory for valuing employee labor. The rates of pay, both in absolute terms and in terms of differentials, are state-controlled. Both productivity levels and labor scarcity are allowed to dictate advantages in wage and salary differentials, in money plus a wide range of fringe benefits. For the rest, differential levels are established in accord with general ideas of supply and demand attaching to given occupations as seen by government economists aided by official trade union leaders. These mechanisms are similar to those posited in

---

[4] What contemporary Marxist theory notably fails to take into account is that in industrial nations today nearly everyone is an employee, including the heads and top management of most large enterprises, both public and private. Are these the new working class? It would hardly seem so, yet they are all certainly involved in the great unrest over differential pay levels.

classical economic theory, except that shifts in differentials are brought about by governmental coercive power rather than by collectively organized coercion.

Thus it is that Marxist political economy, just as classical political economy, fails to provide an adequate theory of equity in wage and salary differential distribution. The spread of wage and salary levels from bottom to top of the incomes ladder is not openly debated; and the differential structure is subverted by special fringe benefits for officials and other members of the party elite, including cars, apartments, special shopping facilities, and other benefits.

It will be evident from the foregoing that it is unlikely that classical or Marxist economic theory will provide much help with solving the vexed problem of differentials. As mentioned above, even in the work of Keynes, who was perhaps more aware of the significance of the problem, there is no reference to any means of overcoming it. Let us therefore return to the issues raised at the beginning of the previous section, and outline how the problem must be turned round and transformed.

The first thing is to treat the problem of achieving an equitable structure of wage and salary differentials in its own right and for its own sake. Given such a state of affairs (and I shall describe how it may be achieved) it would become possible to have full employment without stimulating self-perpetuating wage—push and salary—push inflation. If that fact is not self-evident, evidence will be produced to support it in Chapter 6.

How to achieve abundant employment through demand-side measures is established in Keynesian economics. The problem has been how to do so without inflation and without excessive public borrowing. Again, so long as there is nationwide equity in differentials, and the consequences of malignant instability in differentials are thus avoided, it can be shown that a nation can be helped to face up to the question of the standard of living it can afford because it knows how to distribute that standard of living equitably.

If it is possible to have abundant employment without cost—push inflation by means of establishing an equitable distribution of wage and salary differentials, it then remains to settle the optimum political means of economic organization of trade in goods and services. That question will be addressed in the next chapter. Then the questions of full employment and equitable pay differentials will be considered in turn, not as economic regulators but as prime and independent political objectives.

PART TWO

POLITICAL PLURALISM, FREE ENTERPRISE, AND EMPLOYMENT

CHAPTER 3

Competitive Free Enterprise

The concept of the market in economics is commonly divided into the concept of the commodity market and the concept of the labor market, both supposedly subject to the laws of supply and demand. The principles of functioning of supply and demand on the commodity market are generally understood. They are not understood for the so-called labor market; and labor economics remains the most dismal area of the dismal science.

The reason that our understanding of the economics of supply and demand in the labor market is in an unsatisfactory state is that the very concept of a labor market is itself an untenable and unworkable idea. By contrast, a freely competitive commodity market founded upon pro-ducer−consumer supply−demand relationships is a realistic and essen-tial institution for a democratic industrial society. These views will be considered in this chapter. My objective in so doing is a limited one. It is to establish how, in private enterprise commodity marketing, the differential values of commodities relative to one another are set by the relative preferences of consumers. These differential relative values for commodities vary with changes in priorities in consumer preferences. This freedom of variation of commodity values relative to one another is to be sharply contrasted with the pattern of differentials or relativities in employment wages and salaries, which do not vary freely. Wage and salary differentials are strongly tied to differentials in levels of employ-ment work and not to consumer (employer) preferences; and this work−pay relationship is distorted and disturbed if allowed to be subject to market forces.

Identifying the possibility of having a real and free commodity exchange market and the impossibility of having a free labor market makes it possible to establish the profound differences between, on the one hand, the valuation and pricing of goods and services and the consequential valuation of the activities of self-employed entrepreneurs, and hence their incomes, and, on the other hand, the valuation of employment work, and hence the wages and salaries of employees.

These distinctions point to the profound policy differences called for in a democratic industrial society, between commodity pricing (free-ranging), entrepreneurial profit and loss (free-ranging), and employment wage and salary differentials (not free-ranging but distributed equitably in accord with differentials in work level).

Political Pluralism

Since we shall be concerned only with the conditions that must be established for a requisite political economy—that is to say, a political economy which spreads trust and reduces cause for suspicion among people, supports an all-round sense of fairness and justice, and encourages social adaptation—it is necessary to indicate briefly the underlying political conditions to be assumed. The prime conditions are those familiar as democratic functioning. There must be freedom of thought and association, and the conditions which come with political pluralism. Individuals must be able to set up whatever political parties they wish, to formulate whatever policies they deem to be necessary, and to pursue those policies by due argument and persuasion.

We shall rely upon these processes for settling the levels and differential distribution of wages and salaries; that is to say, it will be a central feature of this argument that public debate and democratic political processes should be established as the means of determining the pattern of relative socioeconomic status to be distributed within the employment sector, and that the power bargaining that is supposed to be the expression of a labor market but is in fact nothing more than naked coercion, should be discontinued.

These political conditions will be much easier to achieve if the political economy can be got right, especially with respect to equity and justice in income distribution. It is the shortcomings in our theories and principles of political economy which prevent us from achieving an equitable distribution of socioeconomic status and relativities in industrial societies. The resulting alienation and disaffection are a constant threat to confidence in democratic values and institutions.

Utility Valuation as Consumer Preference

Here, in summary form, are some of the main features and major advantages of a freely functioning competitive commodity market.

There is no way in which any hierarchy of differential prices of goods and services relative one to another can be construed as objectively attributable to some inherently fixed hierarchy of goods and services. The prices at which goods and services are actually sold move up and down relative to one another, depending upon their supply and the needs, desires, and preferences of the consumers who compete for them. I am referring purposely for the moment to relative prices and not to general levels of market price, since there are other factors besides free market forces which may push general price levels out of line when compared with consumer preferences and relative valuation.

The relative valuation of goods and services by consumer preference must prevail in a free and just society. There are two exceptions to this rule, both of which serve to prove the rule itself. The first is that if there are goods and services which constitute a threat to the very existence of a society, then they should not be available in the marketplace. The second exception is that if goods or services necessary for individual survival are in extremely short supply, they may be rationed at a controlled price.

Apart from these exceptional circumstances, it is dysfunctional to restrict the free choice of individuals to seek and obtain goods and services in accord with their own personal preferences. These preferences will vary from person to person; it is unlikely that any two individuals will have the same hierarchy of relative preferences at any given time. In no way, therefore, can the preferred needs of individuals be provided by centrally controlled planning (other than in a siege economy).

What is required, as a matter of filling the minimum social-psychological requirements of a good society, is the existence of free trading relationships between willing sellers and willing buyers. That is the limiting case for achieving the nonexploitative noncoercive relationship in which, as Adam Smith pointed out, everyone gains—seller and buyer alike. It follows from this that if consumers are to have a reasonable freedom of choice, there must be reasonable freedom for those who provide goods and services to do so in accord with their best judgments of consumer needs and desires. Those judgments involve the balancing of strength of consumer preference and demand against the likely costs of satisfying that demand.

It is a sine qua non, therefore, of satisfying market preferences that there should be a free-enterprise competitive market. It is such a market that provides consumers with the opportunity to express relative preferences in their choice of the goods and services which they actually purchase at given prices. It is also such a market that rewards most highly those providers of goods and services who serve the social function of having a sound sense of what consumers want and need, and who are competent at satisfying those needs.

Constructive Competition

There has, of course, been a reaction against competitive free enterprise, and competition per se is often enough considered to be a
destructive human emotion: competition as a human value suffers badly
compared with the value placed upon cooperation. This generalized
downgrading of competition is unfortunate and unrealistic. Our attitudes
are overly influenced by our experience either of competition directed
solely toward the destruction of the other, or of pseudo-competition, of
competition in an unfree market (for example, competition undermined
by monopoly control or by lack of availability of seed capital or venture
capital). They are also overly influenced by confusion between competition in the provision of goods and services to consumers (which can be
constructive and anti-exploitative) and competition in a labor market to
pay the most to get hold of employees or to see who can pay the least
(which is inevitably destructive and exploitative and, as I shall argue,
ought to be eliminated).

The understanding of the goods and services which people need, as
well as the ability to design and to produce and to offer those goods and
services, is a most creative and constructive human endeavor. This
endeavor is often regarded as of subsidiary importance to efficient
production and good engineering or design for their own sakes. Sales
and marketing, by comparison, are too readily downgraded as marginally nonutilitarian, as applying pressure to an otherwise unwilling
market.

The fact is, however, that all provisions of goods and services,
regardless of political economy—whether capitalist, or socialist, or
mixed welfare, or other political mixture—always as a matter of basic
principle comprises three main interlinked activities; namely, the development, the provision, and the sale of those goods and services
which have value to that market at a price at which it is profitable for
them to be offered. Central to those three activities is the requirement
that the goods or services should be attractive to customers at the
offering price.

The catch, of course, is that it can never be known in advance how
attractive any particular goods or services will be, what the volume of
the demand for them will be, and how long that demand will last before
it is replaced by a preference for something else which is offered—at a
lower price, or with more desirable features, or as a complete substitute.
There must be enough producers who are willing to risk the uncertainties of the market in developing and bringing forward a sufficient range
of goods and services to allow preferences to be expressed.

The marketing of goods and services is a risky business. But so is

everything in life. There can never be certainty about human preferences. Even the air we breathe, the water we drink, the food we eat, and
the clothes we wear—all absolutely essential for remaining alive—are
readily subject to variations in individual preferences in how they are
presented—in preferences for smoking or nonsmoking areas, bottled
waters, and an enormous range of choices in food and clothing, all of
which are now reflected in the marketing of those products and services.

Who then is to say what the public wants? Who is to decide what
public preferences and tastes actually are, as against deciding what the
public ought to want or what is good for it? The answer must be to leave
it to creative individuals who think that they are able to sense and judge
those needs, with the freedom to put those judgments into effect, and,
most important, the willingness to accept personally the consequences of
their judgments in personal gain or loss.

The freedom to put these judgments into effect raises the prime
economic question: who is to provide the investment necessary to
design, produce, and offer goods and services to a market? It is
necessary that someone should forego satisfaction for the time being and
invest savings in such an enterprise. Such investment may be privately
provided by way of individual risk—or it may be governmentally
provided by way of spreading the risk over the total population. The big
political question is which in principle is likely to prove the most
satisfactory. Or to put this question another way, are there any tenable
arguments as to why any individuals who think they have something of
value to produce and to offer on sale to others, are willing to invest in
their judgment, and to put that investment at risk, should be precluded
from doing so? In order to consider the matter, let us first review certain
elementary features of the nature of commercial enterprise.

Individual and Corporate Private Enterprise
It is essential to recognize the distinction between two main types of
private entrepreneurship in modern industrial societies: individual private entrepreneurship and corporate private entrepreneurship. Individual
private entrepreneurship is that in which ownership and directorship are
one; a trader puts up his own personal resources in time and money, and
receives earnings only if the income from his own enterprise exceeds his
expenses—the true and original concept of profit and loss. Such a
private entrepreneur may or may not employ others to work for him.
Even when he does have employees, he himself provides the active
working leadership—as owner-director-manager. Examples are the privately owned farms, shops, and businesses which are mainly small
so-called one-man businesses but may range to some very large family-

owned businesses, and all private professional people such as doctors, lawyers, architects, and others in private practice.

Corporate private entrepreneurship, by contrast, is that form of enterprise in which ownership is in the hands of a limited liability shareholding association hoping to get a return on capital investment, separated from the directorship which it elects and pays a fee.[1] The investors are widely spread and are liable only for the amount they have invested as shareholders. The directors are elected from among the shareholders, and they also are liable only to the extent of their personal shareholdings. They in turn employ chief executives to conduct the affairs of the business through employee systems which may consist of anywhere from a handful to hundreds or thousands or hundreds of thousands of employees. Some, or all, of the directors may also be appointed as executive employees, for which duties they will be paid a salary.

The significance I wish to draw from this distinction between individual and corporate private entrepreneurship lies in the differences between the entrepreneurial risks and the rewards involved. In individual private entrepreneurship, the entrepreneurs invest and risk their own personal resources, or obtain loans or other forms of credit in order to do so. They will receive an income only if their income on trade is greater than their expenses. They know personally, in a very telling way, the meaning of profit and loss. For profit, if any, is what they have available not only to replenish resources and to develop, but also to be drawn from in order to live. Many private entrepreneurial partnerships, indeed, use the term ''drawings''—that is to say, what they draw from the till each week—to refer to their earnings.

In corporate private entrepreneurship, by contrast, the shareholders risk only their financial investment; their just reward is a fair return, so long as the business is trading successfully, for the degree of risk they have accepted and for foregoing expenditure and use of the money they have invested; this fair return must include proper adjustments in line with any general inflation of wage and salary incomes. The directors receive in addition a fee for determining the policies of the company and overseeing the activities of the chief executive and employees. But chief

---

[1] Legislation in Great Britain over the period 1825–1856 gradually granted limited liability to most types of company. The great debate on the subject was at its height during the late 1830s, the time of the railway boom. There was initially bitter opposition from many quarters on the grounds that such an innovation would encourage rash speculation and fraudulent promotions. Eventually, the Limited Liability Act of 1855 and the Joint-Stock Companies Act of 1856 established most of the present-day practice in the United Kingdom.

executives are employees receiving salaries—although if, as may often be the case, they are also directors and shareholders, they will receive fees and dividends (if any) as well. No one, however, in the case of a corporate private enterprise can dip directly into profits as personal income, as is the case with the individual private entrepreneurs who, if they choose to do so, may use all their profits for their own personal incomes.[2]

A major difference, then, between individual private entrepreneurs and incorporated entrepreneurs is that the private entrepreneurs are running personal businesses with personal risk, and are not holding resources in trust for others. The directors of corporate private entrepreneurships, by contrast, are in positions of corporate public trusteeship: it is the corporation, the institutionalized group, which is the "I" and not the identifiable private person as himself or herself.

The individual private entrepreneurial undertaking is open both for risk and for income. It is up to the personal entrepreneurs to run their businesses on the scale their individual capabilities allow. The rewards for success are potentially high, whether in the case of business owners, or professionals, or artists of various kinds who achieve public popularity. It is no use, however, decrying the high incomes earned by some of those individuals compared with the wages and salaries earned by employees, since there is no guarantee either of continued high earnings or of any earnings at all. High earnings one year may be followed by low earnings or even losses the next. That is the nature of the game.

The incorporated entrepreneurial setting is different with respect to income. The rewards may be lower, but then so are the risks. For the rewards are spread more widely, and so too are the risks—spread over shareholders, directors, and payments to employees. No one person or family takes the full brunt of profit or loss. It is the more anonymous entity, the corporate body, which does so. That fact has implications for the responsibilities of directors and for the payment levels of senior executives, which will be considered later.

Self-Employed Incomes and Employee Earnings Contrasted

There is widespread confusion and lack of clarity in public policy and in economic thought about the incomes of entrepreneurs, especially indi-

---

[2] Peter Drucker has put forward a view which I have long held, namely, that the concept of profit is a misleading concept for incorporated businesses. It suggests the existence of a sack of money constituting the undistributed profits, put away somewhere in a vault, and up for grabs by the shareholders, the directors, and the employees. Peter Drucker, (1981), *Management in Turbulent Times*. London: Pan Books.

vidual self-employed entrepreneurs, the wages and salaries of employees, and corporate profitability. Because totally different policies are relevant to each, it is essential to be absolutely clear about all three. In particular, little distinction is made between the earnings of the self-employed and of employees[3]—they both tend to be regarded simply as earnings, and are called by the same name, income.

As a result, there is a failure to discriminate between wage and salary earnings and self-employed profits and losses, and the boundary line between wage and salary earnings and profitability gets blurred. Argument then tends to polarize into two opposing, and equally unrealistic, alternatives: on the one side, it is held (correctly) that entrepreneurial incomes must be left freely open to competition, and that therefore (incorrectly) wage and salary incomes must be left open to competition, because all earnings are basically the same; on the other side, it is argued (correctly) that wage and salary competition tends to be uncontrollably coercive and inflationary, hence some form of incomes policy is necessary, and hence (incorrectly), since incomes are incomes, the policy control must be imposed indiscriminately upon all earners, employees, self-employed, and corporate alike. Thus it is that incomes are nearly always associated with prices in prices and incomes policies, since policy-makers seem to think that in stemming inflation it is only fair that all earners should be controlled to the same extent.

A moment's consideration, however, shows up the profound difference between the role and the incomes of self-employed entrepreneurs and incomes of employees. Let us first be clear about the members of the two groups. The self-employed entrepreneurs include: the self-employed private owners of farms, shops, and businesses; the professionals and semiprofessionals in private practice, individually or in true partnerships—lawyers, doctors, architects, consultants, therapists, beauticians—and those involved in other personal services, such as plumbers, decorators, electricians, carpenters, gardeners; and professional artists and athletes working on their own—musicians, writers, actors, painters, dancers, singers, baseball, football, and tennis players, prizefighters, cricketers.

By contrast, the employees include everyone on open-ended employment contract working in an employment system for a wage or salary, whether in industry, or commerce, or central or local government departments, or in health or education or welfare services, including: manual workers of all skill levels; clerical and other office staff; managers from the lowest management level to the top executive level;

---

[3] See footnote 1, Chapter 2.

scientists, technologists, and technicians at all levels—in engineering, metallurgy, chemistry, physics, mathematics and statistics, operational research, computer sciences; and administrators and specialists in finance and accounting, and in personnel and industrial relations.[4]

The first thing to be noted, as has been stated above, is that the personal income of the self-employed entrepreneur depends totally upon the ongoing profitability of the business or of the practice. It is determined by how much the entrepreneur decides to take for his or her personal use after all expenses have been paid and after allowances have been made for depreciation and replacements and repairs, as well as for any investment in further development of the enterprise. If there is no running profit, the entrepreneur will have to borrow to live. There is no depending upon an employer to get the necessary funds as would be the case for a person in employment.

The entrepreneur's personal income may thus be subject to considerable fluctuation from week to week, month to month, and year to year. Sometimes these fluctuations may be enormous, with huge incomes one year and little or no income, or perhaps a loss, the following year. The incomes of employees do not fluctuate in this manner. Except for ill-conceived attempts to make employees into entrepreneurs by such methods as piecework bonuses and sales bonuses, wages and salaries are constant week in and week out, and change only with merit increases, upgrading, or promotion or a general wage rise.

The level of income of entrepreneurs is decided by what price their goods or services can fetch in the open market, and by what quantity of their goods and services they can sell. That market is made up of myriad potential customers and clients, to whom the entrepreneur is continually appealing—whether by advertising, or public relations, or reputation spread by word of mouth. There is nothing untoward about entrepreneurs negotiating sales with potential customers and clients while at the same time fulfilling contracts or services to existing ones,

---

[4] It is equally important to note who, in the United Kingdom at least, are not included in either of these categories: namely, university academic staff (as against administrative staff); members of the clergy as against church administrators; senior National Health Service hospital doctors; judges; elected political representatives and government ministers. None of the members of these categories is either in an entrepreneurial role or in employee status. For reasons discussed in Jaques, (1976), *A General Theory of Bureaucracy,* their roles and conditions are those of special members of associations, and are not to be confused with either entrepreneurship or wage and salary employment. If we are to sort out the politics and economics of free enterprise and fair employment, it is essential to be crystal clear not only about how they differ from one another but also about how they differ from other types of work role. To advance in understanding will require the utmost precision in formulation.

and having as many clients as they can handle. Employees, however, settle contractually with one employer, and as long as they are working they do not advertise their skills to other employers unless they wish to change employment. They certainly do not have as many employers as possible at the same time. Nor do employees have to seek orders to keep themselves occupied. It is for the employer to get the orders to keep the employees occupied, and to supply the premises and equipment and raw materials.

Finally, self-employed entrepreneurs can charge whatever price they like for their goods and services. There is no question of fair and just comparisons with the prices set by competitors. No entrepreneurs, or groups of entrepreneurs, are entitled to approach their customers and potential customers and complain that they are not being paid enough as compared with others. Nor can they get together and leapfrog their prices above others—not without being guilty of creating price rings and illegal restraint of trade. If there is any legal counterpart of wage and salary leapfrogging, it is an upside-down counterpart: the leapfrogging is downward in the sense of competitive price reduction.

Commodity Prices and the So-Called Price of Labor

This downward movement of prices under the impact of genuinely free competition toward the lowest level consistent with minimally profitable trade in an open supply–demand market is precisely the opposite of what happens to employment wage and salary levels; the latter move inexorably upward.

The major reasons for the profound differences in the way commodity prices move, as compared with movements in wage and salary levels, can now be seen: the commodity market is a market in which relative prices and trade are dictated by the interaction between consumer needs and preferences, and the costs at which producers can fulfill the needs. There are no price differentials which are objectively structured in the articles. Any given product in a particular consumer field may, for example, hold a relatively unpreferred position as compared with other products in the same field. Then, as a result of change in consumer taste and preference it might move higher in the preferred list, and if it has no substantial competitors its price might be able to be increased relative to other commodities. Such changes, and I emphasize again that I am referring to changes in the relativities or differentials in prices, are not the occasion for charges of differential unfairness or of collective negotiation to increase the prices of related commodities. That is not what market trade is about.

Employment roles can be seen to be quite different. No true

marketplace with day-to-day open trading exists. There is no page in the daily financial press showing up-and-down movements on the labor market for the previous day in the offer and buying prices of diecasters as compared with typists, or first-line managers, or computer operators—for there is no such open trading market (and if there were, it would be a slave market). And changes in the wage and salary differentials between occupations without any manifest equivalent differential change in level of responsibility most decidedly do become occasions for charges of differential unfairness, and the source of what is experienced as justifiable social unrest.

The fact is that whereas there can be and are true market mechanisms for the exchange of goods and services, there is not, and cannot ever be, a true market for the sale and purchase of labor in employment hierarchies in employment societies. The concept of the labor market is a misconceived formulation of what is objectively possible: it is a misleading concept. A free competitive market mechanism in the sense of a trading relationship between a producer (the employee?) and a consumer (the employer?) cannot exist. Wage and salary employees work in structured employment hierarchies, with roles ranging from higher to lower levels of work. The hierarchical structure of differential pay corresponds to the hierarchy of levels of work more or less independently of the differential conditions of supply and demand. The differential pay structure is thus a firm objective property of the hierarchical work situation and is resistant to the shifting tastes or preferences of individual consumers.

The true nature of wage and salary differentials, and the fallacious concept of the labor market, will be further elaborated in Part Three (Chapters 5 to 8). Commodity price levels, and the related entrepreneurial profit and loss levels, are entirely different from wage and salary levels. They must be left free to operate under market conditions, because that is the only guarantee of freedom for the members of a democratic industrial society to satisfy their personal preferences in goods and services within the limits of the realities of the availability of resources.

The State Corporate Alternative

Are there, however, any reasons in principle why government departments, functioning like large incorporated monopoly entrepreneurships, should not provide what the public wants, and without what many would regard as the unseemliness or ugliness of economic competition for personal profit? There is a very important reason in principle, and it is the same as the reason why private enterprise monopolies cannot be allowed. In this analysis I exclude, of course, what I would call the sovereign services; that is to say, those governmental activities that are an integral part of the sovereign duties of the state: the institutions of government itself, the tax authorities, and the agencies and services concerned with the criminal legal processes; the services concerned with the control of the national boundaries, such as the foreign service, defense, immigration, tariffs, and customs; and the government services connected with standard-setting and with inspectorates to ensure on behalf of the public that those standards are maintained in such services as health and education, environmental control, factory and office conditions, safety in building and other construction. It should be noted that these services are not competitive activities provided for a market: they are to sustain the intactness of the nation.

In addition, there will be special circumstances where governments—both national and local—will have to provide some non-sovereign services. Such services might include basic provisions in health, education and family social services, or transportation and other services which for particular reasons are not adequately covered in some local region. These services must always be kept open to competition. They would in any case be kept from self-protective proliferation in a nation which had eliminated extremes of poverty and social deprivation because its people were abundantly employed and enjoyed an equitable differential distribution of wages and salaries.[5]

The reason why free competition is essential is that a consumer's decision to purchase particular goods or services is a specific identifiable act. It may be an act carried out within some policy, but it is not in itself a policy. Now, consider the process by which a government monopoly (or any monopoly) must decide what goods or services to provide. Market surveys may be carried out—but they are far from telling what consumers will actually do: the survey results must always be interpreted by the entrepreneur. In the end, either one responsible individual or a committee must decide what to produce, in what range of quality and design features, and so on. That decision is a policy decision. It sets the sole policy within which particular goods and services are offered to the market. Because it is the sole policy it tends to the provision of aggregated rather than disaggregated goods and services.

---

[5] In addition to the safeguarding of free competition, it is always necessary to prevent over-manning in governmental employment systems, by means of sound management. Because these systems are financed by taxation, and their managers are not subject to the stringent discipline imposed by having to rely upon income earned from a market, sound management is not always easy to provide. How abundant employment can set the stage to overcome this problem is referred to in Chapter 4. It is a matter which I have dealt with in detail in *A General Theory of Bureaucracy*.

The critical point is what happens when differences of opinion arise during the decision process among those involved in constructing the decision. For differences of opinion there certainly will be. It is a proper part of the policy-making process to iron out those differences, and either for a committee to arrive at a consensus or for a responsible executive to decide between alternatives.

What usually happens in this process is that the differences of opinion are decided in committee and smoothed out in a policy on behalf of the consumer, rather than allowing individual consumers themselves to have free choice between the various alternatives considered and to buy this or that. In short, the only choice for the consumer is to have a policy item or nothing at all; that is the consequence of aggregation of commodities.

The question, then, is who is to choose? A committee setting policies on behalf of all consumers? Or individual consumers making individual choices on their own behalf? And a related question is who is to decide what to provide: a committee risking the public's capital raised by taxation and without any competition to judge the committee right or wrong? Or individuals risking their own personal capital or private capital which they hold in trust, and with market competition by other like enterprises to keep their judgments of human needs constantly under pressure?

The fact is that there is no substitute for the sharpening of individual judgment by individual accountability and individual financial risk. A powerful sense of responsibility and concentration of attention results from having to put one's own personal reputation and private resources on the line with respect to one's decisions which will be challenged by competitors in an open market. It is quite different in quality from making decisions which will remain unchallenged by competitors. The competitive test is a psychologically most significant and constructive social arrangement for reinforcing all the natural concern for what might be the real needs of others, the needs which they are willing to give economic priority to satisfying. It is a matter of enlightened self-interest on both sides.

Besides the elimination of personal competitive testing, state ownership of all provision of goods and services has a second important consequence. It puts everyone into employee status whether they like it or not; every working member of society becomes an employee in an employment hierarchy, and without even the freedom to choose whom to work for.

To force employment status on everyone, and to leave no opportunity either for personal private enterprise or for investment in incorporated private enterprise, is to put an unnecessary and stressful restriction upon citizens. It restricts the individual initiative of those who believe they have goods or services to offer to the market which fellow citizens will want. It restricts the consumers' freedom of choice and it substitutes the clumsiness, and the tendency toward insensitivity produced by the featherbedded security of noncompetitive government monopoly.

There is no substantive reason for imposing such monopolistic governmental restrictions on a nation. The choice between being an employee and an entrepreneur must be kept open—open, however, so long as there are abundant employment opportunities and equitable payment for those who choose to be employed. These prime conditions for democracy in industrial societies will be considered next. But first, one final word on free enterprise is called for.

Freedom to Employ—A Social Privilege

Competitive free enterprise refers to the freedom of entrepreneurs to decide what they shall offer into the commodity (goods and services) market, and at what price; and the freedom of customers and clients to decide what they shall buy at any particular moment in time, and at what price they would be willing to buy it. It depends upon freedom of competition among a multiplicity of entrepreneurs, and freedom to bid and buy among a multiplicity of consumers. Competitive free enterprise, as defined here, does not include the misleading conception of free competition in an open and free labor market.

I have argued what to many will seem an argument for free enterprise that really needs no arguing. Others, opposed to private enterprise, will consider it a sham social psychological apologia for capitalism. It is intended to be neither. What I seek to do is to lay a foundation for socially responsible employment of fellow citizens both by private entrepreneurs and by government in the sovereign services on behalf of the people. But it is not employment under any old conditions. The right to employ others, whether by the community through government or by entrepreneurs, must be recognized for the great social privilege it is.

It is a commonly held view, however, that exploitation of labor is an inevitable consequence of free enterprise, and that the elimination of exploitation requires the elimination of free enterprise and the substitution of state ownership. In fact, exploitation is just as readily produced under nationalization or complete government ownership as under private enterprise. Governments acting in the name of the "people" are just as capable of exploitation of the people as are private entrepreneurs. The elimination of exploitation lies not in getting rid of free enterprise.

It lies in providing employees with the freedom of movement engendered by abundant employment, and in removing the settlement of wage and salary differentials from spurious market mechanisms; and substituting democratically determined differentials related to differentials in level of work, regardless of who the employer might be.

There must therefore be an adequate and firm context for employment, whether in private enterprise or in public service. It is the task of society as a whole, and not of employers, or employers and employees in coercive power negotiation with each other, to decree the prime conditions of employment, including the differential levels of payment for differentials in level of work. That issue and the matter of ensuring that there shall be an abundance of employment are matters of far too fundamental importance to social life and political cohesion in industrial societies to be left to any individuals or subgroups. The privilege of employing others, and of being employed oneself under equitable conditions, must be paid for by adherence to a properly regulated context. It is this context, and its safeguarding of freedom and justice, to which I shall now turn.

CHAPTER 4

Abundant Employment

Competitive free enterprise is essential if people are to have the freedom to choose how they will live their lives, and if reward is to be given to those who are willing to risk being entrepreneurs and who best understand the needs and preferences of others and are capable of producing goods and services to satisfy those needs at prices which are acceptable relative to other prices. Entrepreneurs must be free to profit or lose by their activities, in free and open competition with others; this competition is the moving force toward consumer satisfaction and reasonable pricing.

Most entrepreneurs have to set up employment systems large or small, and have to employ people on wage or salary in those systems, in order to get their work done. The status of employee, however, will have to be recognized as being absolutely different in kind from that of entrepreneur. In the twentieth century, in industrial employment societies, an abundance of employment opportunity must be continuously sustained and assured throughout the whole nation if society itself is not to take on a bitter taste for everyone.

The concept of abundant employment must be sharply distinguished from that of full employment. The term 'full employment' will be used to refer to there being some kind of employment role available for everyone who seeks employment—not necessarily of interest, not necessarily up to one's level of capability, and not necessarily near at hand geographically—but at least a job for a wage or salary. The term 'abundant employment' will be used to refer to there being employment available for those who seek it—at least of some interest, mainly within daily travel distance, and decidedly at a level consistent not only with a person's level of capability but also with a person's growth in level of capability.

Every employment nation must muster and nurture the most sustained political will to maintain abundant employment. For there are no economic barriers to abundant employment, only political barriers. Unemployment is necessary only if those who are employed are unwilling to share the burden of adverse economic conditions with those who are not employed. It is a political problem of distribution and not of economic depression. I propose to show how this problem of distribution can be resolved by equitable differentials in income distribution, and abundant employment maintained.

It will be argued, therefore, that democratic employment nations must establish nothing less than the absolute constitutional right of their citizens to freedom of enterprise, abundant employment, and an equitable distribution of wage and salary incomes. Nothing less will do.

The Open-Ended Employment Contract in Employment Societies

As I mentioned in Chapter 1, the twentieth century has seen the emergence of the employment society in industrialized nations. In considering full or abundant employment it will be necessary to establish the nature of employment itself in such societies. Employment in the modern sense is based upon the widespread application of the late nineteenth-century development of what I termed the open-ended contract. This contract has the most powerful positive and negative consequences. Let me develop further the theme introduced in the earlier chapter.

The open-ended employment contract is a contract in which an employer takes on an employee to carry out an agreed type of work or range of tasks, in return for a wage or salary[1] under specified working conditions, the contract to run indefinitely unless terminated by a specific act of leaving by the employee, with due notice, dismissal by the employer, for due cause of negligence or incompetence, or declaration of redundancy by the employer.

The contract is for a specified weekly-hours period (say a 35- or 40-hour week) at a location and with equipment and materials provided by the employer. The employee lives at home and not on the employer's

---

[1] The cause of understanding is not helped by the current widespread use of the term salary to refer to monetary payments in roles that are not in employment systems; the 'salaries', for example, of university academic staff, clergy, members of Congress and Parliament. Once they are all referred to as salaries, it is assumed that they can be paid in accord with the same principle. But in fact, the basis of payment of an elected representative (an honorarium reflecting public esteem), academic staff (a stipend reflecting corporate involvement in the life of the university per se), and clergy (a 'living' which represents both Church membership and total commitment of self to the worshiping community), is significantly different in each case, and all are vastly different from the basis of payment of salaried employment. I would press for some such usage as: fees for directors; earnings of entrepreneurs; wages and salaries (or salaries alone) for employees; honoraria or fees for elected representatives; stipends for academic staff and for clergy.

premises. The open-type of contract thus excludes all casual day work, migrant labor, self-employed craftsmen (the guild members), the gangs and gangers in mining, and live-in domestic workers (who constituted about 15 percent of the work force in England in the nineteenth century and who were governed by the law of the so-called master—servant relationship).

This type of open-ended contract is modern. In the case of manual workers, it replaced the day-by-day employment in which tomorrow's job was always in doubt (a condition which persists, for example, for dock labor in many ports), or the true piecework (payment by the piece) of a cottage industry. It was introduced into the textile industry in England during the latter half of the nineteenth century, and has now become the standard form of employment worldwide, in industrial nations and in the industrialized parts of the developing nations. It applies in all employment: industrial and commercial; federal, state, and local government; and education, health, and social services.

The significance of the open-ended employment contract is that it removes the last vestiges of any entrepreneurial content of employment for a wage or salary. It encloses employees within employing enterprises, and, so long as they have a job, removes them from the so-called labor market. Entrepreneurs are never removed from the day-to-day cut and thrust of their market—not without ceasing to be entrepreneurs, that is.

It is the open-ended contract which also establishes the special nature of unemployment in employment societies. Unemployment and employment are not shifting hour-by-hour day-by-day states, stopping and starting, without either continuing security or insecurity. They have become much more extended quasi-permanent states. To get a job is far more than having yet another day's work, and more than yet another job or contract for an entrepreneur. It is the achievement of pro tem security without a known end-point, a security which may extend no one knows how long into the future.

This feature of open-ended longer-term security in employment roles has undergone remarkable extension during the past 50 years. There is legal protection against unfair dismissal. Redundancy must be argued out, and employees in the advanced industrial nations are mostly covered by redundancy pay arrangements—an expression of the emergence of the principle that employees in general terms are entitled to continuation of employment. And in countries like Japan and India, employers have been made legally responsible for providing life-time employment for many categories of employee.

This twentieth-century development is one in which manual work changed from day work for the unskilled and the semi-skilled, and entrepreneurial self-employed work for the skilled craftsman and artisan, to continuous engagement in a career in employee status.

The consequences of this development for a profound change in the meaning of unemployment will be obvious. Unemployment comes to refer to a potentially chronic state of affairs, in which no work at all is available, or will be available until the unemployed person succeeds in finding a new open-ended employment role. People in these circumstances may attempt to fill in with day-to-day jobs, but that, however successful, is in no way equivalent to finding employment in the modern sense.

The crucial significance of abundant employment in modern employment society becomes evident. In most Western industrial nations over 70 to 80 percent (and in England and the United States over 85 percent) of everyone who works for a living does so under open-ended employment contract in an employment hierarchy, in work which constitutes a potential life-time career. This work cannot be changed from day to day. Nor can the pay contract be changed from day to day. We are dealing with a socially persistent state of affairs, a weighty socioeconomic relationship with powerful momentum. It must be considered in its own right, with its own properties to be understood.

In long-term careers and their development, people need to have the opportunity to achieve levels of employment consistent with their levels of capability, and growth in opportunity matching growth and development in levels of capability. That is what abundant employment means, as against merely some kind of employment for everyone. The citizens of an employment society are unlikely to tolerate for any length of time a state of affairs in which adequate opportunity for individual career development does not exist, or is not reasonably assured.

Abundant Employment a Constitutional Right

In the light of the foregoing consideration of abundant employment and unemployment, it may be self-evident why abundant employment must be regarded as a constitutional right of every person in a democratic industrial employment society. By a constitutional right I mean just that. No nation should have the right to industrialize, with the inevitable emergence of an employment society, without undertaking at the same time to guarantee abundant employment, in the same way that it must guarantee equality of educational opportunity or just treatment under the law.

For once a nation has become industrialized, to work for a living will, in the case of most of the working population, require that they do so by gaining employment for a wage or salary in a job in an employment hierarchy. To have less than an abundant employment opportunity—that is to say, to be either unemployed or underemployed—has two intensely disturbing effects: one is the effect on the employee; the other is the effect on employees' attitudes toward employers.

Unemployment and the fear of unemployment are both psychologically debilitating and socially alienating.[2] They induce chronic depression and despair, emotional disturbance, and understandable delinquency and criminality, especially in young people. And underneath all, the strongest feelings of suspicion and mistrust of society are aroused and become permanently fixed.

Less well recognized is a crucial accompanying consequence of unemployment. Those who are employed increasingly become underemployed as time passes, since it is difficult if not impossible to gain the opportunity to progress so as to maintain a level of work consistent with one's maturing level of capability. Even with full employment there may be gross underemployment, for example, in areas dominated by industries providing routine jobs with low levels of work, as in many mass production industries and routinized commercial offices. Chronic underemployment produces the same effects in psychological depth as unemployment. For anyone to be forced to work at a level below their full capability, 40 hours a week, week in week out, for possibly a lifetime, is psychologically devastating. No decent society is entitled to do that to its people.

The accompanying effect of underemployment is true exploitation of employees. The employers get the advantage of higher levels of capability than are warranted by the levels of work and payment they are offering. The employees feel exploited and resentful.

It is no wonder in such circumstances—and they are very widespread in capitalist industrial societies—that disaffection is widespread and becoming increasingly so. It is a deep-seated malaise, and one regarding which socialist nations have an advantage: they approximate

---

[2] These effects have been documented during the 1930s and corroborated by later researches which showed the effects to be similar to other experiences of loss. There is first what amounts to a denial of the situation, with an increase in activities such as house repairs and decoration, car maintenance, etc. Then there is increasing distress as the ex-worker fails to regain employment and experiences increasing poverty and the inability to provide for his family. Then finally there is despairing resignation and adjustment to an unemployed style of life: job seeking and social interests are curtailed, and most of the time is spent at home or even isolated from the family circle. M. Jahoda, P. Lazarsfeld and H. Zeisel, (1933), *Marienthal: The Sociography of an Unemployed Community.* London: Tavistock; and P. Eisenberg and P. Lazarsfeld, (1938), "The Psychological Effects of Unemployment," *Psychological Bulletin,* 35, 358—90.

more closely to abundant employment. The price they pay, of course, is having to suffer under autocratic corporate state control, with some direction of labor as in most East European countries. The question for the democratic industrial world is how to achieve abundant employment without state corporatism and without one-party, often military, suppression. If it is not achieved, the immediate future for the democratic industrial world is bleak.

No Economic Barriers to Abundant Employment
Attempts have been made to increase level of work in some few enterprises by means of so-called job enrichment programs. These programs, however well-intentioned, are of minor importance, partly because they affect so few people, partly because they do not deal satisfactorily with individual cases, partly because they do not provide for some of the very extensive increases in level of work that are required, and partly because they are confined to shop- and office-floor roles whereas underemployment occurs at all levels.

More substantial attempts to create abundant employment are inhibited by two false arguments. One argument is economic: abundant employment cannot be afforded, requires excessive increases in the supply of money, breeds inflation, and reduces labor mobility. The second argument is technological: productive efficiency is said to call for the greatest possible rationalization of production methods, and if the ensuing work is beneath the competence of the workers then the thing to do is to compensate by moderately higher pay than the work warrants.

Let me examine both these fallacious lines of thought.

The first fallacy has been called the "lump of labor fallacy." It is the notion that there is a finite limit to the amount of work available in a locality or in a nation or in the world. From this point of view there will be less and less for people to do as the available work runs out, mainly by being transferred to machines and robots. Therefore, or so runs the argument, the workweek will have to be steadily reduced (to what point no one quite states), people will have to be "trained" to use more leisure, youngsters will have to be kept longer in school (even though they may hate it), and in general everyone will have to get used to working less and less or perhaps even to never working at all.[3]

The fact is, however, that there is always enough work in any nation to occupy all its people fully for as many hours a week as is thought desirable. This proposition is self-evident, despite the above

---

[3] The "lump of labor fallacy" was completely exploded in *The Economist*, January 8, 1981. But it continues to hold a strong grip on the public imagination.

widespread notion that current developments in technology will render many people unemployed for life unless there is to be a very short workweek or people retire very early. Technological developments do make it possible to get many jobs done by machine. But that just means that people are freed to do the jobs that people do best—for example, in health and the hundred and one other services that have always been underprovided—and the transition to what Daniel Bell has called the postindustrial society. It is often said, of course, that those services are not wealth-producing. But what does that mean? It is a statement that equates real wealth solely with physical products. That is a terribly limited view of life and human value!

Nor need abundant employment breed wage— and salary—push inflation. That is a question of being able to deal rationally with wage and salary differentials so that any economic hardship can not only be equitably distributed and shared but can be seen to have been shared in this way. It will be shown in detail in the following chapters how readily that can be done; and how readily the general level of wage and salary incomes can be adjusted so as to be kept in line with that standard of living that the nation can afford.

As for increasing government expenditures, causing more money to be printed, and increasing the national debt, abundant employment need not inevitably have any of these effects. The real problem is a political problem of level and distribution of wage and salary incomes. The question is whether those who are employed are willing to share so that those who are unemployed can be effectively employed rather than paid marginally less on unemployment welfare for doing nothing. Abundant employment combined with equitable income differentials achieves precisely the effect of making sharing possible without inflation.[4]

Here is an issue of national cohesion, of national morale. A nation cannot turn its back upon its unemployed and underemployed. It is an

[4] The opposite, and socially iniquitous, process is dramatically and concisely expressed in the following editorial view which, while referring to Britain, must be seen as a foretaste of the future for all industrial nations: "This helps to explain Britain's odd recession. As measured, real gdp—meaning volume—appears to have fallen faster than at any time since the war; and unemployment hits one record after another. But consumer spending has stayed remarkably buoyant. With real wage rises under their belts, those still in employment have done nicely, thank you." *The Economist,* December 27, 1980, pg. 11.

This statement is an accurate indictment of current theory and practice. It was written at a time when the British government was grimly hanging on to a policy which counted upon intolerable levels of unemployment to bring the employed to heel and to get them to give up their demands for pay increases. The most paralyzing thing is the degree to which people accept the idea that this way of running a nation is inevitable under free enterprise.

insult to everyone. We must make up our minds to use our greatest asset: our human talent. What has become a cliché has to be transformed into hard reality.

Finally, it is a mistaken idea to argue that the national economy demands that the most economic means of production must be used regardless of the types and levels of work which result. The survival of democratic industrialization requires a technology which in general terms provides a distribution of levels of work in employment which matches the distribution of levels of capability in the population. That is the import of abundant employment. Chronic deviation from this state of affairs will simply continue the accumulation of disaffection with employment until all our democratic institutions are undermined. That process is manifestly already well advanced.

This problem of matching technological efficiency to the levels of capability of the people is best dealt with by abundant employment. In these circumstances people have the opportunity to move if they are not satisfied with the level of work they have. Production technologists have little difficulty in modifying production methods to meet the requirements and skills of the people available. Assumptions about the available labor have always been built into production technology as one of the crucial factors in designing productively efficient methods.

Underemployment of people due to the production technology used is possible partly because people are forced to accept such work and might otherwise face the risk of unemployment. But there is another supporting factor in the idea that it is all right to underemploy people so long as you pay them well. This idea is the second of the two fallacies: the fallacy that work is merely instrumental, and that people do not mind what they do so long as they can earn the money they require.

Widespread underemployment of people with overpayment may endure in the short term. But in the middle and long term it is possible only if there is a background threat of unemployment. Sustained underemployment produces psychological and social disturbance whatever the pay. The enjoyment of the money undermines morality, for it is getting something for nothing, and people know it; and those in other occupations with higher levels of work but the same pay bitterly resent the inequity—hence, for example, the periodic eruption of differentials disputes between miners and automotive assembly-line workers. At the same time the hatred of the work and of being incarcerated in it, and of having sold out one's creativity and capability, stirs the rage and hatred toward both oneself and the society which produces such a humanly disreputable condition. A steady accumulation of social and political stress is inevitable.

Modes of Achieving Abundant Employment

A nation that is suffering unemployment is a nation whose standard of living is lower than it ought to be, lower than it would be, that is, if everyone were fully at work. Every democratic society must realize and accept the fact that its survival as a decent, free, and just society demands as an absolute right that there shall be abundant employment, that everyone shall know that there will be abundant employment, and that the only question is how to make it possible at any given time.

The main requirement for maintaining abundant employment is to recognize that it is a political problem and not to be afraid of it. The second requirement is to ensure a steady supply of investment capital to maintain a buoyant economy at a standard of living which the nation can afford. It will be shown in subsequent chapters how the available national standard of living can be faced and fairly shared so that a nation can be sure of continuously paying its way. Before turning to these issues I shall briefly review a series of policies for overcoming temporary periods of unemployment should they occur.

The first thing to be achieved is a national willingness to share the available standard of living equitably. How that can be achieved is the subject of the following chapters. Under these conditions, the foundation is set for an all-round sharing of whatever standard of living is available—even if it is a reduced standard—so that everyone is in the same boat and everyone can work. Under these conditions the Keynesian demand–pull solution to achievement of abundant employment can work: government investment in private growth enterprise; temporary improvement of socially valuable services, as in health and housing; and the use on a local government basis of stockpiles of useful local improvement work set aside to be carried out in just such circumstances.

Such programs may require extensive retraining opportunities. But retraining programs in turn provide employment and training occupation, and reduce unemployment. As a result, they cost the nation little if anything; by equipping people with employable skills, the national treasury is saved the cost of unemployment benefits and in due course receives the taxes paid by the reemployed.

So long as the differential payment structure is perceived to be fair and equitable, such programs of distribution of work and redistribution of income are feasible without inflation or increased borrowing or sale of national resources. A nation that is unable to face such a situation, given the means to do so, is a nation that is ill and divided. Truly equitable sharing in adversity, in a socially healthy nation, should be a source of strengthened national morale and national determination to get back to a sounder and stronger economy.

But surely, it may be argued, there must be some cost to be faced for having abundant employment. That view is incorrect in a fundamental sense. No nation can be worse off for having all its people at work than it would be for having many of them idle. Abundant employment of its citizens must bring both greater economic output and the incalculable gain of a cohesive and mutually trusting population, as against a divided population with an alienated and mutually mistrustful outlook.

There is a lesser sense, however, in which there are costs to be faced. But those costs are in redistribution of income and choice of personal expenditure. In practice the redistribution of income might amount to a reduction of some 5 percent for those in employment to make up the difference between the welfare benefit received by unemployed persons and the wage or salary they would be receiving once they were employed. This 5 percent is not, however, physically lost: it is lost only in the sense that there is a loss of personal choice of expenditure on bought goods and services, balanced by a gain in governmentally provided free goods and services; that is to say, the price paid by the nation is a slight loss of economic freedom of choice by the employed so that everyone can be at work. In the end everyone gains.

The risk in such a policy is that there would be a growing governmental provision of services over and above the sovereign services, with after-tax wages in the private sector shrinking progressively. Any such eventuality needs to be explicitly guarded against. The essential control is to stimulate growth in the private sector to absorb those temporarily employed in the non-sovereign government services. The very fact that such employment is only temporary needs to be made explicit and manifest: long-term employment security must be made to reside in the private sector and the sovereign services.

There is of course the more general criticism that any policy which increases governmental employment will lead to inefficiency and waste because governmental organizations tend to employ more people than they need. In my experience, it is not necessarily true that governmental organizations are badly managed. But even where they are, the proper solution is not to have unemployment and then to use the existence of unemployment to swing an undiscriminating axe on government employment; that is a cowardly and socially disruptive way to deal with the accumulated effects of chronic bad management. The proper solution is to sustain abundant employment, and to maintain continual pressure in all employment systems, governmental and private alike, to prevent over-manning and featherbedding. That is a matter of ordinary sound management.[5]

In short, a combination of Keynesian and monetarist demand management and supply-side measures stands a much better chance of preventing unemployment and controlling inflation if the following conditions are met: there is a strong national determination that no citizen shall suffer enforced unemployment and idleness; there is an agreed and acceptable differential payment policy in the nation; payment for abundant employment comes not from printing money, or borrowing, or selling off national resources, but from the nation's being willing to accept income redistribution as between the employed and the otherwise unemployed; there is a national will to accept the standard of living that the nation can afford at any given time; and there is an acceptance of the principle that government services, other than sovereign services, will be only temporary. These conditions are all essential and they are interdependent: any nation which would spurn them is entitled neither to economic security nor to the benefits of human freedom and justice.

Mobility, Welfare, and Redundancy

Given abundant employment, what ought the policy to be for those who do become temporarily unemployed or who do not choose to take advantage of abundant employment opportunities? And, what do employers do in growth enterprises to attract employees when there is an abundance of employment available everywhere? How is labor mobility to be sustained?

Given an abundant employment political economy, it is reasonable to expect that individuals would work for their living, either at a level consistent with their capability or at a lower level if they happened for their own personal reasons to want to do so. Our definition of abundant employment here becomes politically significant: each person is entitled to employment, and must be willing to accept it, at a level consistent with capability, in line with experience and knowledge, at an equitable differential pay level, but not necessarily in line with primary interest unless willing to move.

Under these conditions people who become temporarily unemployed should be entitled to welfare at the level of pay of their last job.

[5] The fact that assured abundant employment is an essential condition for sound organization and management of employment systems is a theme which I have elaborated in *A General Theory of Bureaucracy,* op. cit.

If retraining is called for, that also should be at the same level of pay. But from the moment that appropriate levels of work become available, that welfare payment level should rapidly and radically reduce, and continue to do so until whatever is deemed to be subsistence level is reached.[6]

The net effect of such policy would be to provide full protection of standard of living for those who wish to work but temporarily have become unemployed. At the same time, it would allow those who wish to opt out and not to contribute to the general economic welfare by their work, to subsist.

By the same token, with abundant employment, redundancy takes on a different emotional tone. It would be an expression of loss of employment in a particular place and perhaps of particular interest, but not unavailability of employment per se. Redundancy payments would therefore be related to loss of individual convenience, but not as a buffer against economic insecurity and risk of long-term unemployment. These payments would be directly related to length of service. They would on the whole be smaller than the present trend toward the large payments which are meant to assuage society's guilt about the prospect of someone's being put out of work for a long time. Many people now seek redundancy as a means of getting a financial nest egg by capitalizing upon that social guilt.

The issues of business contraction and unemployment raise a series of related questions about how employment systems must requisitely be managed, especially in connection with the contraction of businesses. Those are questions which I shall simply note at this time, and turn to in Chapter 10.

What then about the question of retirement age? Given abundant employment there is no reason why people should be forced to retire before they want to. Many people are continuing to advance in level of capability well past the age of 65. Perhaps with lessening of energy older people who wish to continue to work could be placed on lighter duties, or part-time duties, practices which are in any case not uncommon. Retirement age would be a technical matter of the minimum age at which pensions rights could obtain for those who wished to retire, and not a mandatory deprivation of employment.

Finally, there are the questions about labor mobility under abundant employment. They will be addressed in Chapter 9, after procedures for effecting wage and salary differential equity have been described—to which subject the next section is devoted.

---

[6] I do not propose here to enter into the general field of allowances for children and other dependents, but am assuming that they would be treated separately from wages and salaries, as direct social payments explicitly for the use of dependents.

PART THREE

EQUITABLE DISTRIBUTION OF WAGES AND SALARIES, AND THE DIFFERENTIAL CONCERTINA

CHAPTER 5

Employment and Payment Differentials

It will now be necessary, if our argument is to proceed, to consider and to question our assumptions about human nature with respect to some of the most pervasive and dynamic processes in industrial societies. This has to do with our assumptions about what is human work, why we work, what makes us work; then with our assumptions about what we expect from work, what we expect to be paid and why; and then with our assumptions about our feelings of fairness and unfairness in pay, especially our feelings about income distribution and egalitarianism and inequality, and whether the achievement of an all-round fair and just distribution of income might ever be a realistic goal in a democratic society.

These questions take us into the heart of some of the fundamental differences between classical and socialist political economic theory, between capitalism and Marxism. Both of these themes can be shown to be based upon inaccurate assumptions about human nature and values. They are about half right and half wrong. Classical theory is right with respect to the competitive commodity market, but wrong with respect to the labor market; Marxist theory was right to try to eliminate employee exploitation, but wrong in eliminating competitive market mechanisms for commodity exchange. The widespread use in society of the theories built upon these partly false assumptions has intensely disruptive consequences: coercive use of power, manipulation of people, economic inequity and injustice, and a waste of human talent and ability.

An alternative theoretical position will be built upon a pattern of findings derived from extensive practical field work over many years, with systematic studies at all levels in employment systems—those social systems which assume such a dominant position under industrialization. These findings established a precise definition of the nature of human work, and led to an objective measurement of level of employment work—in terms of the objective assessment of the time-span of discretion required in each employment role. This measurement in turn provided the tools necessary to reveal the existence of a deep and previously unrecognized sense in people about a fair differential distribution of wages and salaries uniquely related to differentials in level of work measured in time-span. These widespread feelings could then be seen to be the expression of extremely powerful systems of norms and values about what a fair and equitable differential distribution of wage and salary incomes should be within a nation.

It is the existence of these systems of felt-fair wage and salary differentials which makes possible a political economy in which wage and salary levels can be treated independently as a social and political objective with its own economic instruments. In the following four chapters the findings will be outlined first; then an instrument for formulating national wage and salary policies—the differential concertina—will be described; and finally, the use of the differential concertina for fixing and modifying nationally both the general levels and the differential distribution of wages and salaries will be demonstrated.

In the final section of the book, the argument will be pursued to show: first, how a political solution to the fixing of wage and salary levels and differentials supplies the so far missing, but absolutely essential, base for sustaining abundant employment with the complete elimination of any consequential wage—push and salary—push inflation; and second, how the combination of a publicly determined wage and salary equity, and assured abundant employment, are necessary conditions for safeguarding competitive free enterprise without employee exploitation, and with guaranteed freedom for productive entrepreneurship and for the expression of consumer choice. The connection with the achievement of genuine equality of opportunity in industrial employment societies will be considered.

The Employed and the Self-Employed

The assumptions about human work and labor which underlie capitalist economic theory (and most other economic theory as well) are that work by and large is doing something which you would rather not be doing but which you do because there is no other way of gaining a livelihood. Work is seen as instrumental—as an unpleasant activity carried out in someone else's time which is the means of getting the income necessary for doing in your own time what you want to do. Social theorists do not tend to think this way about their own work, but they do so about the work of those others who are looked upon as less fortunate and have to take jobs in employment systems, especially at shop- and office-floor level. In these latter circumstances it is often argued that incentive bonus payments may be needed in order to persuade people to tolerate the unpleasant activity and do enough work.

Given this conception of work, the employee is seen as engaging in an exchange contract with the employer under which he gives up his time and freedom and contributes his labor, but for a price. The price is determined in the way any other price is determined—as a matter of ordinary bargaining and negotiation. The price will depend on what the market will bear—on what the employer is willing to pay in the light of the available supply of labor and on what the employee is willing to accept in the light of demand for his or her labor.

In short, it is assumed that human labor should be valued in the same way as any other goods and services. It is a matter of utility, of the value established by supply and demand in a freely competitive market. A creative artist's earnings will thus be higher than a manual worker's if the artist's star happens to be in the ascendant. If, however, the artist's popularity wanes, then the income may dwindle and fall below that of the manual worker. So too should the manual worker's income oscillate (although of course it does not) as his or her utility waxes and wanes, and the employer should have to decrease and increase the wages and salaries he pays to his employees. That is the way of the market.

It is recognized that the existence of trade unions may distort the process of bargaining in a free market. But since trade unions are inevitably here to stay, collective bargaining has to be absorbed into economic theory as part of the market mechanism for determining wage and salary levels.

This view that employees will value their own labor in terms of a commodity which they possess and which they can exchange for whatever is the going price in the marketplace is wide of the mark. It fails to take into account the fundamental difference between employment for a wage or salary and individual free entrepreneurial activity.[1] Let me complete the task of making this distinction absolutely clear.

Pay Differentials and Employment Systems
The self-employed entrepreneur—the singer, the actor, the lawyer, the doctor, the owner of a business, the architect—have all set themselves up in business to trade in a free market. That is why they can be registered as companies. No one is employing them on a regular

[1] Marx, of course, did make the distinction between the workers and the owners of the means of production. This distinction tends, however, to be restricted to private ownership of companies and manual workers. It fails to cover the limited liability company, in which everyone but the shareholders is an employee. The problem of income differentials today is to take account of the profits (or losses) of private ownership and of self-employment, and of the enormous range of wage and salary incomes from shop and office floor to middle managers, professionals and technologists, as well as the top executive levels.

open-ended employment contract. They establish themselves in business or in private practice, and take their day-to-day risk of continuity of business. No one else is getting work for them (unless they themselves employ an agent) and employing them to do it. No one else is worrying about how to get the money to pay them. They have to worry for themselves about what they ought to be doing to follow trends and ups and downs in the market. And their business incomes and expenses go up and down day by day, week by week, year by year, with no way of knowing what those incomes and expenses are likely to be at any given time.

To be an employee is something quite different. It is a status that has yet to be taken adequately into account in political and economic theory and in law. The vast majority of employees are on open-ended contract, as defined in Chapter 1, to work for a wage or salary, not *as* a company but *for* a company or other employing institution.

The negotiated payment for open-ended contract employees does not go up and down with the availability of customers for the company by whom they are employed (other than by overtime or short-time work); it is the employer's earnings which do so. The employee does not have to find the money to pay the wages or salaries; it is the employer who has to do so. The employee does not risk going out of business; the entrepreneurial employer does. And finally, the biggest difference of all lies in the fact that an entrepreneur has access to a free market in the sense of being able to have and to bargain with a multiplicity of clients or customers all at the same time; open-ended contract employees have only one employer, and if they wish to change employers they are involved in a complex process of leaving one job, transitional unemployment, and finding another job.

In short, the open-ended employment contract leads to an entirely different socioeconomic status from that of the individual entrepreneur and his actual and potential customers or clients. It is a quasi-permanent status, in which the employee has entitlement, in ordinary circumstances, to continued employment.

The gravamen of this distinction between individual entrepreneurial work and the open-ended employment contract work is that entrepreneurs not only accept but welcome an oscillating free-market valuation of their work. They take the personal risks but stand to gain a great deal if they happen to be able individually to satisfy their impersonal multi-client market and obtain a great demand for their work. Employees, however, are in an entirely different position. They are being employed at a level of work fixed by their employer. There are other employees working at the same level and at higher and lower levels in the same establishment. Here the whole question of reward becomes not what an entrepreneur individually can squeeze out of an impersonal market in day-by-day offering of goods and services, but rather what are the differentials appropriate to the various levels of work in employment hierarchies. These two questions are different from each other.

In short, each negotiation of an entrepreneur is a negotiation with a client or customer for the supply of particular goods or services in competition with other entrepreneurs in an impersonal free market in which they can in most cases openly offer and advertise their wares. In contrast, the negotiations of employees are concerned with improving their positions by obtaining increases in reward not from a market but from their sole current employer.

There are economists who decry this situation and would have it that each employee should act as an individual entrepreneur and negotiate with any and all employers, as though there were a free market composed of all employers. But this viewpoint overlooks the realities of the nature of employment work and the fundamental difference between being a self-employed entrepreneur and being employed by an entrepreneur. There is no way in which the open-ended contract of employment in an employment system can be made to conform to entrepreneurial self-employment.

The payment levels in open-ended employment roles are determined within the hierarchical structure of the employment systems. In broad terms, the wage and salary levels increase with increases in level in the hierarchy—ranging from the so-called unskilled levels at the bottom through semi-skilled and skilled levels, and then up through the various managerial and specialist levels to top management. The pay levels are fixed, either as flat rates or within narrow brackets, for the positions and not for the individual incumbents of the positions.

What individual employees negotiate for is not a price or fee for each contract; they negotiate for a particular position—that is to say, they apply for a job. If they get the job they get the rate of pay that goes with the job. If they wish to seek an increase in pay they may attempt to do so either by seeking a pay increase within a bracket for merit or length of service or by seeking to gain career progression by means of upgrading or promotion. This process is in sharp contrast to entrepreneurs, whose clients have no responsibility whatever for giving them a periodic merit review or for their career progression.

The problem of wage and salary levels per se, then, is not an individually negotiable issue. It has to do with the setting of pay levels for given levels of work in employment hierarchies. That is a very different issue from an individually negotiable contract. It calls for some method of categorizing employment work in relation to levels within employment hierarchies. Such methods have so far proven elusive. They must not only be applicable for establishing relative levels between positions within the same employment system; they must also be able to compare the levels of positions in different hierarchies, because employees in similar categories of work, or even in different categories, do make these comparisons. It is contrary to entrepreneurial competition, for entrepreneurs to cry "unfair" if a competitor gets a higher price or sells more cheaply; it is an inherent property of the social structure of the employment situation for employees not only to feel fairly or unfairly treated relative to other employees, but to express those feelings in industrial action.

The main methods for sorting out wage and salary levels and differentials have been fragmented collective bargaining and various types of job evaluation, or combinations of both. The inefficacy of these methods, and the painful cost of this inefficacy in pay leapfrogging and wage-push and salary-push inflation, have been considered in Chapter 2. Let us turn, therefore, to an entirely different method of handling this problem and an exploration of the consequences for political economics of doing so.

CHAPTER 6

Time-Span Measurement and Equitable Pay

It has been argued that competitive free enterprise is a necessary condition to allow for realistic expression of consumer preferences for goods and services, and for establishing the differential utility of goods and services at any given time. Free enterprise—both personal and incorporated—can be a constructive social force of great power so long as four main conditions are in operation: abundant employment with equitable payment for employees; no restrictive monopoly; governmental administration supplied by government; and essential services protected by government.

The most difficult of these conditions to achieve is that of an equitable wage and salary distribution for the vast array of employees with widely varying levels of responsibility. Politically, there are two problems which have to be solved. The first is how to settle and to modify as much as is necessary the general level of wage and salary payments. The second is how to settle and to modify as much as is necessary the differential relationships among wages and salaries. There have so far been no procedures for achieving these ends by open democratic political means. The coercive methods which are in use are exceptionally disruptive of political relationships and the economy.

The underlying problem is how to determine what should be paid for in employment, and what should determine relative levels of pay. A radically different approach to solving this problem will be described. It is a practical approach, and certainly less difficult in application than the bewildering complexity and confusion of the methods presently in use.

It should be pointed out, however, that even the consideration of these proposals, never mind their possible implementation, would require the strongest political will. For the open and direct consideration of differentials is among the most distasteful of all political issues. It requires that a nation should publicly address itself to the domineering and explosive question in employment systems of who should earn how much as compared with others. Should there be differentials? If so, why? Should there be equality? If so, why? The disturbing issue of the distribution of relative socioeconomic status is at stake. Very few people are tempted to rest their own personal case for an income the same as or higher than others on public debate, and to rely upon rational debate to settle the matter. They are justified in such an attitude so long as there is no reasoned foundation for such a debate. This chapter will outline precisely such a foundation.

Let me therefore come to the central feature of my argument. It is the feature whose absence has made both classical and Marxist political economies unworkable in the advanced industrial nations which have become employment societies. It is a method for determining a manifest and agreed differential distribution of wage and salary incomes, and for adjusting it so as to keep it in line with changing values of what would be a fair and just spread of differentials in socioeconomic status related to differentials in level of employment work.

In the succeeding chapters it will then become possible to show how this method of handling income differentials makes it possible to maintain a continuous state of abundance of employment without contributing to an insidious wage—push or salary—push or to excessive and uncontrollable inflation; this, in sum, is the best guarantee of a just and healthy free enterprise.

Time-Span Measurement and Level of Work
The following findings, based upon thirty years of practical field research, demonstrate that employees at all levels have a sense of fairness and justice with respect to differentials in their wage and salary earnings; moreover, this sense of fairness has never been realized or taken into account in economic, political, or social theory. The main finding is quite simple, and is as follows: regardless of their actual pay levels, and regardless of their assumptions or knowledge about the market value of their work in relation to supply and demand, *employees who are employed at the same level of work have the same standards of what would be fair payment for that work.*

This finding holds for all employees regardless of occupation or level: in industry, commerce, public administration, and social services, on the shop and office floor; middle managerial, professional, and technical; and higher managerial and executive. To put it another way, employees at the same level of work name the same felt-fair pay. This finding holds nationally in countries the size of England or throughout the major industrial regions of larger countries such as the eastern seaboard in the United States.

In order to make such statements it is necessary to define wage and salary incomes with precision. These terms will be used to refer to total emolument for a standard workweek (that is to say, without overtime or other premium payments) including money payment plus the actuarial value of special emoluments in lieu of money, such as provision of cars or housing, special tax breaks or health and life insurance policies, or share options.

The central question, of course, is how common levels of work can be measured so that they can be compared with the judgments of individual employees as to what constitutes felt-fair pay. This problem was solved by the discovery of a unique relationship between what I have called the time-span of discretion in each employee's role and the felt level of work in the role. The measurement of time-span is derived from the fact that when a subordinate receives an assignment (whether directly from his manager or from some other authorized source) a maximum target time by which the assignment is intended or planned for completion is always set. This maximum target completion time may be either explicitly stated or implicitly understood, but it is always there; it may be actually achieved, or not achieved, or altered: but at the moment of assignment it always exists.[1]

The time-span in any role is derived simply by establishing with a manager and a subordinate those assignments or sequences of assignments that have the longest maximum target completion time. This period expresses the maximum periods of time during which managers target their subordinates to exercise adequate judgment in balancing pace against quality in their work—to do work of sufficiently good quality quickly enough.

The following are brief examples of time-span measurement of a number of roles. They are intended only to illustrate the nature of time-span in employment roles, and not as a treatise on the method of time-span measurement. They are examples of actual roles, and are not hypothetical constructions: it is no more possible to measure the time-spans of hypothetical roles than it is to measure the lengths of hypothetical pieces of string.[2]

---

[1] The method of measuring time-span in employment systems and the results of doing so, with several hundred examples, will be found in Elliott Jaques, (1964), *Time-Span Handbook*. London: Heinemann Educational Books Ltd., and Southern Illinois University Press; and in John Evans, (1970), "Time-Span—The Neglected Tool," *Personnel Management,* February 1970, and *The Professional Engineer,* Vol. 15, No. 2, May 1970; and (1979) *The Management of Human Capacity.* Bradford: MCB Publications. The background of the method is described in Jaques, (1961), *Equitable Payment.* London: Heinemann Educational Books Ltd.

[2] The argument that this form of measurement is totally objective and akin to ordinary derived measures in the physical sciences, and based upon simple extensive measurement, is set out in Jaques, (1982), *The Form of Time.* New York: Crane, Russak and Company, Inc., and London: Heinemann Educational Books Ltd., Chapter XI.

One point of absolute practical significance must be emphasized. The time-span measures described are for specific individual roles, and cannot be generalized to other roles of the same job title. The notion that all jobs of the same title carry the same level of work, and that therefore all jobs of the same title should carry the same pay, is one of the great fallacies in employment systems. It is simply not the case that any positions called secretary, or semiskilled lathe operator, or tool-maker, or automobile assembly-line worker, or foreman, or diecaster, or motorman, or teacher, or nurse, or coal miner, or truck driver, are at the same level as all other positions with the same title. Nor is it the case that the pay of miners as a category can in practical and realistic terms be compared with the pay of nurses, or of foremen, or of any other general descriptive category of jobs grouped under the same title because they encompass activities of broadly the same type.

In short, job titles tell something about the kind of activity to be found in a role. They do not, and cannot, tell the level of work in the role. Jobs with the same title can carry very different levels of work. It is heading for confusion and trouble, therefore, to try to establish the rate for the job where "rate for the job" refers to a rate for a job title rather than the rate for each particular position or role. In the policy to be outlined, the rate for the job refers to the same rate for all positions in the same time-span range, *regardless* of type of work or title.

The time-span of discretion in a role is defined as: the maximum period during which an employee is targeted to exercise discretion, within prescribed limits (policies, rules and regulations, tolerances) in balancing pace against quality (that is to say, to work quickly enough and to the required standards of quality). In each of the examples below, the time-span is stated as the longest period that could elapse before a manager could be sure that the work of a subordinate was not just marginally substandard in quality or just getting marginally behind in time.

Lathe operator—metal manufacture: turning metal components to fine tolerances, in batches requiring from 2 hours to 2 days, in accord with detailed drawings. Up to a maximum of three days of output could be produced before any of the work necessarily arrived at a quality review point. Time-span: 3 days.

Another lathe operator in a different department in the same factory was doing turning work on batches of rather larger components which took longer to do—from half a day to up to a week. Nearly two weeks at a maximum could elapse during which none of the output was checked for quality. Time-span: 2 weeks.

(Two roles: same titles; same activity; different time-spans of discretion; different levels of work.)

Invoice clerk: checking invoices on export orders. Expected to clear 45 to 60 invoices per day. Discretion lay in keeping the pace at the maximum rate consistent with not overlooking mistakes. Inexperienced clerk whose work was spotchecked by a supervisor at least once per day. Time-span: 1 day. Experienced clerk, whose documents were not rechecked until export documentation process was completed up to a maximum of two weeks later. Time-span: 2 weeks.

Machine tool fitter: final assembly of completed machine tools from subassemblies. Discretion lay in blueing and scraping so that moving parts worked smoothly and kept tolerances. Longest assemblies up to ten weeks. Each machine tool tested immediately upon completion. Time-span: 10 weeks.

First-line manager: had a multiplicity of assignments, and had to exercise continual discretion in determining own priorities. Longest tasks were concerned with the induction training of new staff for a probationary period with a maximum term of four months. Time-span: 4 months. Another first-line manager was responsible for extended training and upgrading exercises for her own subordinates, some of which were programmed over nine months. Time-span: 9 months.

Department manager: managing a department of 280 people. Multiple-task role, with longest assignments concerned with projects for the introduction of specified new methods and equipment, related modification of existing equipment, and retraining of staff, without losing output, such projects targeted for eight to eighteen months. Time-span: 18 months.

Research workers: a research officer had several projects at once, the longest targeted for completion in six months. Time-span: 6 months. A research program manager worked on his own projects with the assistance of research officers, the longest project in the program targeted for completion in fifteen months. Time-span: 15 months. (Note: In both cases, as in all employment in research, the task is to complete a particular study or program in a given time, rather than to make a discovery at some unspecifiable time or other.)

General sales manager: a multiple-task role with assignments ranging from immediate sales discussions with customers to the establishment of a Far East sales network targeted to be in full operation within three years. Time-span: 3 years.

Subsidiary chief executive: was operating within an overall plan calling for a total redirection of the business within seven years, including new technology and new buildings and equipment, and a major shift in product lines and markets. Time-span: 7 years.

Corporate executive vice president: had responsibility for the strategic development of a group of businesses providing services for the retired, including the establishment of up to four new business sub-sidiaries by growth or acquisition, the whole process to unfold in relation to the likely demographic changes occurring over the coming 15 years. Time-span: 15 years.

The above descriptions are highly compressed digests of the most significant elements in these roles from the point of view of time-span measurement. Enough information is provided, however, to illustrate the way the time-span of operation extends with the movement to higher and higher levels in employment hierarchies. At the higher extreme, although a person will have a wide range of short- and middle-term tasks, all work is framed in responsibility for the operation of long-term strategic activity. At the lower extreme, the middle- and long-term tasks are not to be found, the work being confined to single tasks or task sequences of days' to weeks' duration. This pattern of extension of time-span of discretion with movement from lower to higher levels of responsibility is a universal feature of employment hierarchies with wage and salary structures: it is to be found in industry, commerce, central and local government services, and in health, education, and welfare institutions.

Felt-Fair Differential Wage and Salary Levels

The significance of time-span measurement was revealed through the discovery of a unique relationship between the measured time-span of the work in a role and the feelings of the occupant of the role about what would be fair pay for that work: what I have termed the felt-fair pay. People who were employed at the same time-span named the same felt-fair pay, regardless of occupation, job title, actual pay, skill, length of training required, length of service, age, sex, color, complexity, versatility, specialization, physical strength, foresight, intelligence, imagination, or any of the other factors commonly regarded as influencing employees' attitudes toward their pay, including even the three Ds, dirt, danger, and discomfort.

This unique relationship between time-span and felt-fair pay is illustrated in Figure 6.1 in the graphs for England and the United States in 1980. The same differential pattern has been found for England since 1955, and for the United States since 1963 (the dates when data were first obtained), the actual felt-fair pay values moving upward at the same rate as the movement in the earnings index for each country, but independently of changes in the cost of living index. That is to say, employees sense their felt-fair pay levels in comparison with the pay levels being received by others rather than in relation to the absolute value of their earnings. It is how we are doing as compared with others that counts where wage and salary differentials are concerned.

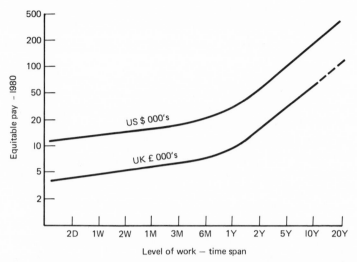

Figure 6.1: Graphs showing pattern of felt-fair pay and time-span in the United States and in England in 1980.

It must be noted that the felt-fair pay levels shown for England and the United States do not necessarily indicate the actual payment levels for given levels of work in the two countries. As will be shown in Chapter 9, in the United States in 1980 actual pay levels were fairly consistent with felt-fair—or equitable—pay; whereas in England there was a fairly close match from about £4,500 up to about £10,000 a year, below and above which levels actual pay steadily fell farther and farther below equitable levels.

The most systematic controlled study of the relationship between time-span and felt-fair pay was carried out between 1964 and 1966 by Roy Richardson at the Honeywell Corporation in Minneapolis, Minnesota.[3] Richardson obtained time-span measures on staff in three different occupational groups—research, sales, and production—at three very different levels in the organization. The time-spans were assessed by students specially trained in the method and provided with previously derived work-study descriptions of tasks as a basis for interviews, but ignorant of the background and purpose of the work—so as to eliminate the possibility of experimenter bias. The felt-fair pay judgments were gathered by means of a simple written questionnaire filled out by the subjects on their own.

In addition to time-span measures and felt-fair pay judgments,

[3] This study was supervised from the University of Minnesota, and published in Roy Richardson, (1971), *Fair Pay and Work*. London: Heinemann Educational Books Ltd.

some 28 other variables were included in the study. These variables covered all the factors which the researchers considered could in any way affect a person's feelings of fair pay for work, and included, where relevant, the judgments of the manager as well as the employee. Thus data were gathered on age, actual pay, length of service, a range of factors from job evaluation schemes such as foresight, judgment, skill, responsibility, numbers of subordinates (if any), knowledge, the judgment of both the employee and the manager of the current local market value of the work.

The results showed a high correlation between time-span and felt-fair pay (0.86) and time-span and actual pay (0.74), with lower correlations ranging from 0.52 (judged market value) downward for the other variables. But far more striking was the finding from a regression analysis of the data that time-span explained 75 percent of the variation in felt-fair pay, actual pay explained only 10 percent, and no other variable explained more than slightly over 1 percent of the variation.

Equally high correlations (0.85) were obtained in a less controlled study of jobs in twelve different firms in the United Kingdom by Krimpas, Evans and Miller in the 1960s.[4] The work varied from that of unskilled manual workers to office staff up to middle managerial levels, in occupations as diverse as steel making, chocolate manufacturing, shoe production, delivery services, and engineering.

In another study, in Holland,[5] comparisons were made between the rank ordering of jobs by time-span measurement and that obtained by judgments of the managers directly concerned, plus a study by job evaluation. The rank ordering by these different methods was close. But more significant was the fact that when discrepancies were reassessed, the managers altered their judgments in the direction of the time-span ordering.

There have been some other studies, however, which might seem to throw some doubt upon these findings. One such study is that of Goodman[6] who studied the relationship between managers' guesses about what might be the time-span in a number of roles which they knew about rather more from job title than from any knowledge of actual task content, and the relative levels of work in the roles. Such studies are vitiated by the fact that no actual measurements of time-span

[4] Published in G.E. Krimpas, (1975), *Labour Input and Theory of the Labour Market*. London: Duckworth.

[5] F.C. Hazekamp, (1966), "Werk, Capaciteit en Beloning in het 'Glacier Project' " *Polytechnisch Tijdschrift*, 6.7.66.

[6] Paul S. Goodman, (1967), "An Empirical Examination of Elliott Jaques' Concept of Time-Span," *Human Relations*, Vol. 20, No. 2, pp. 155−170.

were made. Another study, carried out in England by the Department of Employment,[7] threw up a correlation of 0.32 between the time-spans in a sample of manual work roles. This study was unfortunately limited, however, by the fact that the time-spans were obtained in unfamiliar conditions, with no previous elaboration of the task content of the roles, and with task and time-span data obtained only from the manager without any input from the actual worker. In carrying out time-span measurements, it is essential to be able to familiarize oneself with the general nature of the work being done, and to be able to check both with the immediate managers and the subordinates.

The most systematically controlled studies, then, have supported the accumulating fieldwork experience, in over twenty countries during the past 25 years, of the efficacy of time-span measurement as an instrument for measuring level of work in roles connected with the development of organizational systems and structure. These organizational studies are based upon a universal finding to be described in Chapter 7, of a close association between time-span and levels of organization. They constitute the strongest evidence in favor of the view that time-span provides a direct measure of the level of work in any employment role. Because time-span measures level of work, it is not surprising that it should correlate so highly with felt-fair pay. Employees get paid for their work. The higher the level of that work, the higher the pay judged to be fair; work at the same level calls in justice for the same level of pay.

The Meaning of the Equitable Differential Norms

The import of these findings is that underneath all the bargaining over wages and salaries, underneath the influences of supply and demand reflected in varying degrees of employment and unemployment, underneath all the wrangling over pay, all the restless shifting of pay relativities, all the statuses attributed to the job titles of various categories of employment, the apparent anomalies, the coercion, the envy and resentment, and the intensely felt injustices, underneath all the inconsistencies and seeming irrationality of the system, there is a tough and substantial and highly significant pattern of norms of fair pay differentials. What can these norms mean?

The data accumulated now over nearly thirty years have the most profound significance for psychological and social theory and for political economy. They suggest that human beings, when employed in

---

[7] Sheila Cameron, (1973), "An Enquiry into Time-Span of Discretion and Felt-Fair Pay," Research Monograph published by the Department of Employment.

hierarchically organized employment systems for a wage or salary, are not motivated by selfishness and greed alone, as our behavior in negotiations and power bargaining would make it seem. Moved by such negative feelings we certainly are; but we are moved also by positive feelings of fairness and justice. The trouble is that our current inadequate theories and coercive procedures for settling wage and salary differentials are so disturbing in their effects that they bring out the worst in all of us, including the eruption of all of our most primitive unconscious paranoid reactions. But even this strong disaffection is mitigated by our positive impulses—unless we are driven to rage and despair and breaking point when inequity is pushed too far; similarly, destructive hate may be mitigated by positive impulses in the primitive layers of the mind, and paranoid responses held at bay.

The power of the norms of equity in people must be very substantial to be able to subsist through the day-to-day economic inequity that prevails in industrial societies. How these norms of equity are established remains a mystery.[8] The fact of their existence, however, shows how far people will go in organizing their feelings of fairness and justice. They are able to do so in such a way as to allow them to communicate those feelings to one another by nonverbal means, and to create precisely quantifiable norms of which no one is consciously aware.

Special attention must be called to the nature of these norms. They are pay differentials, not absolute pay levels. The differential pattern is constant: it does not vary with supply and demand, or bargaining, or changes in actual pay differentials. In this regard it differs from the differential valuation of material goods and services. These valuations can change in rank order from day to day, or even from hour to hour, depending upon changes in need or in taste, and changes in supply and demand.

Moreover, it is important to note that the equitable differential norms refer specifically and solely to wage and salary payment in employment systems—they do not refer to the earnings (the profits, if any) gained by the self-employed or by private entrepreneurs. That is to say, the constancy of the differential norms of equity is built up in relation to the hierarchical structure of levels of work in employment

---

[8] One possible hypothesis is that employees compare themselves intuitively with one another in terms of other relative levels of capability, and build norms of equivalent differential pay for equivalent differential capability. But how such a mechanism might actually work is not the least bit clear. See, for example, Jaques, (1961), *Equitable Payment*.

systems and not in relation to the sale of entrepreneurial services in a free competitive market.

Wage and salary differentials in employment are therefore encompassed neither under the classical economic theory of the labor market nor under Marxist theories of labor value and need. They are tied up with norms of distributive justice related to people's feelings to the effect that those who carry the same level of responsibility in employment systems should receive the same level of reward regardless of occupation; and by the same token, those who carry higher levels of responsibility should gain higher economic rewards than those who carry lower levels.[9] These findings about equitable pay differentials can be used as one foundation stone for sustaining abundant employment without wage−push and salary−push inflation, and for achieving free enterprise with justice and without labor exploitation, witting or unwitting.

---

[9] This equitable differential work−payment scale is an actual example of the concept of distributive justice which Rawls attempts to articulate in his theory of justice. J. Rawls, (1972), *The Theory of Justice*. Oxford: Clarendon Press.

CHAPTER 7

Stratification of Human Capability and of Work Levels

Although it is not clear how people are able to arrive at a precise accord on what a fair and equitable distribution of wage and salaries would be at any given time, it is clear that these universal norms of fair pay are linked with great exactitude to common levels of employment work as measured objectively by time-span. That the hierarchical structuring of felt-fair pay was linked to a hierarchical structuring of employment work organization was suggested by another set of findings which emerged from time-span measurements made in employment systems; these measurements pointed to the existence of a basic structure of organizational strata which underlies the structure of all employment hierarchies.

An analysis of the meaning of this basic stratification of organization suggested that it is linked to a series of discrete levels in human capability in work. Each work-stratum was found to comprise its own peculiar types of work, regardless of occupation. The type of work activity at each stratum was associated with its own particular mode in which individuals set about their work.

These findings about the stratification of levels of work in employment hierarchies, and of an equivalent hierarchical stratification of human capability in organizing and in shaping the world of work, can then be linked to the hierarchy of felt-fair pay levels associated with the work levels. This triple linkage of level of work, level of capability, and level of pay, pointed toward a fundamental solution to the problem of fair employment: let our employment systems be organized in accord with the basic work-strata; let there be abundant employment, so that individuals can find employment within work-strata consistent with their levels of capability; and let there be a universal hierarchy of wage and salary brackets tied to those work-strata and derived from the norms of equity.

In order to show how this fundamental solution can be made to work, this chapter will be devoted first of all to a description of the basic pattern of work-strata. That having been done, the particular content of work at each stratum, and the particular qualities of individual capability necessary to do the work at each stratum, will be displayed. Finally, how each work-stratum can then be differentiated into three grades for purposes of individual progression in pay and career will be indicated.

The Basic Structure of Work-Strata

It is a familiar fact that there tend to be too many levels of organization in employment hierarchies—too many levels of management. This malfunctioning pattern of organization is almost universal in every industrial nation. It was discovered[1] that not only was there a right number of levels but this right number of levels was always the same for all employment hierarchies everywhere. If only one managerial role fell between successive boundaries, there then existed the right number of levels and there would be the right distance between managers and the immediately subordinate roles; everyone had enough organizational space in which to get on with his work. By contrast, what was experienced as the wrong number of levels was the situation where subordinates felt their managers to be "breathing down their necks"; or where managers felt their subordinates to be too far below them so that they had to lower their own level of work in order to manage them.

The fact that there was a right pattern of organizational strata seemed clear enough. But that this pattern might be the same for employment hierarchies of all kinds, in all circumstances, everywhere, was established only by means of time-span measurement. What became observable through the lens of time-span measurement was that there were sharp cut-off points or boundaries at 3 months, 1 year, 2 years, 5 years, 10 years, 20 years, and (probably) 50 years. No full-scale managerial roles were found below the 3-month time-span. There then was found in practice to be room for one managerial role anywhere between the boundaries of each succeeding stratum. If there were two managerial levels within any one stratum, organizational crowding was experienced; and three levels produced decided overcrowding.

The significance of these findings has been confirmed over the past

---

[1] The data upon which this analysis is based have appeared in a number of publications. The main reports are to be found in Elliott Jaques, (1976), *A General Theory of Bureaucracy;* in Ralph Rowbottom and David Billis, (1978), "Stratification of Work and Organizational Design," and Elliott Jaques, (1978), "Stratified Depth Structure of Bureaucracy," both in Elliott Jaques, R.O. Gibson and D.J. Isaac, (1978), *Levels of Abstraction in Logic and Human Action.* London, and Exeter, New Hampshire: Heinemann Educational Books; and in Gillian Stamp, (1981), "Levels and Types of Managerial Capability," *J. Mgt. Studies,* 18, 3, 1981, pp. 277–297.

Time-Span	Stratum	Organization Level
	Str-VIII	Super Corporation
50Y		
	VII	Corporation
20Y		
	VI	Corporate Group of Subsidiaries
10Y		
	V	Corporate Subsidiary and Top Specialists
5Y		
	IV	General Management and Chief Specialists
2Y		
	III	Departmental Management and Principal Specialists
1Y		
	II	First-Line Managerial, Professional and Technical
3m		
	I	Shop and Office Floor
1d		

Figure 7.1.   The fundamental organizational levels in employment hierarchies.

fifteen years in a substantial number of reorganizations of employment hierarchies in industry, commerce, and public and social services, in a number of different countries. When managerial structuring is brought into line with the basic structure of work-strata described in the accompanying table (Figure 7.1) an effective, understandable, and controllable executive organization is achieved.[2] The reasons why this pattern of organization connects so directly with human experience of sound working relationships, lie in the fact that there is a unique type of working activity—or level of mental abstraction—common to each

[2] References to this work can be found in John Evans, (1979), *The Management of Human Capacity;* and in Elliott Jaques, (1976), *A General Theory of Bureaucracy,* and (1980), "Essential Developments in Bureaucracy in the 1980s," *Journal of Applied Behavioral Science,* Vol. 16, No. 3, 1980, pp. 439–447.

work-stratum. It is this hierarchy of types of mental abstraction which underlies the hierarchy of work-strata and of equitable pay brackets. In the following section I shall describe these strata in terms both of the mental levels of abstraction and of the work content which obtains for each stratum. The work content will be illustrated in each case both for managerial roles and for specialists without subordinates.

Level of Abstraction in Employment Hierarchies

The conception of an underlying universal structure of requisite managerial organization has been strongly reinforced by the discovery that the tasks which are found within each work-stratum have in common the same general characteristics. These characteristics were first teased out by Billis and Rowbottom,[3] some of whose criteria are used in the following description. In case it should be thought that the organizational structure of employment hierarchies can be of no relevance to wage and salary incomes policy, it is well to keep in mind that such incomes policy has its roots precisely in these employment systems. One of the main reasons for the failure to construct sound pay policies is the almost universal dysfunctional organization of these systems in which such a huge number of human beings is employed.

In considering the following material, it should be noted that there is a marked qualitative shift in the complexity of work with each shift in work-stratum.[4] This increase in complexity makes it possible to encompass a much greater field of activity, that is to say, to encompass marked increases in the scope and scale of responsibility, and hence to work in longer time-spans. It may well be the intuitive sense that people have of these qualitative jumps in complexity, as well as the higher and higher levels of abstraction needed to cope with the complexity, that leads to the sense that differentials in pay levels are called for; everyone gains from the abilities of those whose levels of capability make possible the longer-range contexts within which everyone's abilities are more effectively employed, and without which socioeconomic development would be truncated.

It is because this pattern of levels of abstraction is a universal characteristic of human beings that systematic organization is possible. It is this pattern which generates a constant hierarchy of values for employment work; market forces could not produce this consistent value hierarchy. Traded goods do not have any hierarchy of values inherent in

---

[3] Op. cit.
[4] Gillian Stamp. op. cit., has described how this complexity shows in problem-solving activities.

themselves; human beings most decidedly do, as shown in the following description.

Stratum I. Time-Span 1 Day to 3 Months: Shop and Office Floor. The level of abstraction is that of a very concrete mental output. Mode of work is reflected in a touch-and-feel approach in dealing with problems which are concretely and physically at hand. The person is anchored in rules. Once a task is begun it must proceed without interruption to completion. The task itself must be specified in concrete terms, and only one variable is dealt with at a time. Information must be put in concrete and familiar terms.

The focus is upon each distinct task. Each task is concrete, in the sense that the output can be completely prescribed and, if necessary, illustrated by examples or by drawings. If several tasks are carried out at once—e.g., in multiple machine minding—all must be carried through concurrently to completion. Discretion is exercised in how to proceed with each task.

Stratum II. Time-Span 3 Months to 1 Year: First-Line Managerial, Professional, and Technical. This level is that of the first-line manager of a section all of whose members he knows personally, and whom he oversees directly and continuously. The level of abstraction is that not only of being able to carry out single direct tasks, but also and at the same time of being able to articulate in explicit terms how those tasks may be done. The manager can therefore put together and program a series of direct operating tasks, determine which methods should be used for those tasks, and change the program or methods as may be required by the situation. The greater complexity than at Stratum I shows in the ability to have a basket of problems at one time, to determine priorities, and to deal with them intermittently—that is to say, to start one task and carry it so far, then leave it aside and work on another task, and thus to work through the basket giving priority to one or other task as the total program requires.

The focus of the first-line mutual-knowledge section manager is upon an aggregate of tasks being carried out by immediate subordinates, with special attention to those tasks which are causing trouble. The output is the aggregate of outputs from all the tasks; discretion is exercised in maintaining a section of subordinates capable of carrying out the tasks to be assigned, and in overcoming problems outside the competence of the subordinates. The manager knows at first hand, by continual direct observation of the aggregate of tasks he has assigned, how things are going and where problems are arising. Lateral relationships occur at the working interfaces between sections.

The specialist officer (e.g., Personnel Officer, Economist,

Geologist, Research Officer) would ordinarily have a number of assignments on hand at any given time. He would be expected to deal with each separately. Some of the tasks would last over several months, and he would have to use his judgment about priorities and planning and how best to phase the longer assignments so as to be able to cope with all. The framework would be set for each task, and he would not be expected to extrapolate trends to new tasks or to extrapolate the trends in developing knowledge in his field.

Stratum III. Time-Span 1 Year to 2 Years: Mutual Recognition Management. This level is that of the manager of a department whose members can recognize each other. The level of abstraction is that of being able to mold direct operating tasks and operating methods into a functioning system of direct work, and adjust that system as necessary to cope with change. Because of the sequential ordering of experience, the changing trends in problems can be noted, and changing circumstances can be predicted by serial extrapolation. Resources can then be modified to meet the predicted changes by alterations to equipment, or to people (training).

The focus of the manager of a mutual-recognition department is upon the direct leadership of people in a mutual-recognition situation, and upon the control of the trend of tasks and problems arising in the department, seen as a series; extrapolation from these trends of the likely future situation; and the undertaking of modifications to existing equipment, of training of work force, and of adjustment of work flow, in order to cope with changes in trend and to improve effectiveness of operation. The output is a total physical output per unit of controllable expense per specified period of time; and the discretion is exercised in modifying equipment, people, and work flow, so as to increase output and reduce costs.

The specialists at this level would be principal officers (e.g., Principal Chemist, Principal Economist, Principal Research Investigator, Principal Industrial Relations Officer) who would have a number of assignments at the same time and would be expected to adopt a serial extrapolative approach. They would be expected, in the first place, to keep informed about the trend of developments in their own specialist field, and to extrapolate from that trend to the improvement of ways of formulating problems and of methods of solving them. In the second place, they would be expected to take into account the trend of changes in tasks, and to seek appropriate changes in resources to cope with oncoming problems, as well as to ensure their own training and development as required and to train any assistants they might have.

Stratum IV. Time-Span 2 Years to 5 Years: General Management.
Problems at this level are no longer seen in terms of individual tasks per se—either singly, severally, or serially, but in terms of systems of operation. The level of abstraction is that of being able to take a given system of operations, say a particular production system, and to contrast and compare it with one or other of a series of alternative systems, to determine which system might be the most effective. The person must be capable of sufficient detachment from specific cases to be able to treat them as representative examples of issues calling for development of systems which in turn make it possible to handle direct tasks with greater effectiveness. He must be able to judge when a particular case is significant without having to scan all cases. Examples of alternative systems, or of modifications to existing systems would be: new types of equipment; new organization and establishment; new work-flow policies; new technologies and accompanying methods and retraining of personnel.

The managerial focus is that of the general manager, and is no longer upon direct output tasks (either singly, severally, or serially) but upon the equipment, the organization and establishment, and the work-flow process, in relation to getting the output. Management is by exception, in the sense that specific problems are dealt with in a way that generates improved policies and procedures for handling problems. The output is the ratio of the total output delivered to customers and the total allocatable expense per budget period; and discretion is exercised in the identification of opportunities for increasing profitability by the introduction of new types of equipment, new patterns of organization and establishment, and new ways of planning work flow and stocks; constructing proposals for changes of this kind; and pressing for their implementation.

The specialists at this level would be Chief Officers, Scientists and Technologists (Chief Physicist, Chief Computer Scientist, Chief Economist), and would be expected to tackle assignments from two points of view. First, there is the carrying out of the particular task—a research project, an exploration, a systematic analysis of an issue. Second, the projects or the analyses should lead to the extension of existing principles and policies by means of the development of new applications for them; for example, new ways of using existing engineering knowledge in production; new applications of computer science to process control.

Stratum V. Time-Span 5 Years to 10 Years: Corporate Subsidiary.
The level of abstraction is that of being able partly to redefine one's

own field. Problems at this level are no longer dealt with within a context wholly set from above. The person must be able: first, to define the field of operation for others at levels I V to I; and second, to modify his or her own field of operation within policy. Thus, at this level, specific problems are perceived as opportunities to review the adequacy of the context for the work system, and as indicators of the need not just to extend the context but to change it, that is to say, to change the business outline or other policies governing the system.

The managerial focus at this level is that of the managing director concerned with the entrepreneurial development of a successful enterprise. It is the first level of total business activity differentiated into product development, production, and sales. Production output is seen as a whole in relation to sales and to product development. Lateral and upward contexts are open. Problems at this level are no longer dealt with within a context wholly set from above. The nature of the field in which the managing director is operating is now partly defined by himself: he can modify the boundaries of his business, within policy, and in so doing redefine the work system for his subordinate organization. A significant part of the duty of the managing director is to impact upward in strategic development, including the generation of adequate cash flow and getting a sound return on invested capital.

The work of specialists at this and higher levels would be expected to lead to new scientific and technological knowledge which would extend the limits of the special field; for example, an exploration which adds to principles about the use of atomic physics; a research project in biogenetics which leads to further development of principles in biotechnology; a financial information and control project which leads to new policies on information with respect to return on capital investment.

Stratum VI. Time-Span 10 Years to 20 Years: Corporate Group. The level of abstraction is that of being able to deal with social and theoretical systems as entities. At this level there is a qualitative shift in the nature of the entities from which the world is constructed. Entities now become social or theoretical systems rather than categories of physical things or social events. The person must be able to order (coordinate) such systems in relation to one another.

The managerial focus shifts away from the internal functioning of the individual business to the strategic development of each of a group of strategically connected businesses, in relation to business opportunities and within corporate strategy. The key data are international technological developments, changing and newly emerging markets, and new assets and capital. The output is the translation of corporate strategy into business direction, and the translation of business experience into its strategic implications. Lateral and upward contexts are open in the sense that Stratum VI is part of the corporate collegium (the corporate hierarchy).

Stratum VII. Time-Span 20 Years to (?) 50 Years. The level of abstraction is that of being able to plan and organize work in relation to societal development. Work at this level is that of the corporate executive director, or the heads of large government departments, and is consistently related to a practical sense of developments in societies both locally and internationally, including the interweaving of sociological, technological, and demographic and political developments, and their impact upon human needs and expectations. Leadership is given in corporate strategic development to anticipate these changes and to create new businesses or new activities to meet them in the 20- to 30-year term.

Grades within Work-Strata

It is the fact of the universal existence of these discrete levels of abstraction underlying the pattern of discrete work-strata in employment hierarchies—in industry, commerce, government departments, education, health services, social services alike—that makes a systematic wage and salary policy possible. Equivalent pay levels can be attached to the boundaries of work-strata, to give a basic structure of differential pay that would be the same for all occupations.

This system applies not only to managerial positions but to shop and office floor and professional, technological and other specialist roles as well. Measuring the time-span of any role, regardless of type, makes it possible to assign the role to the stratum between whose boundaries it falls.

Generally, however, these hierarchical work-strata are experienced as too wide for purposes of constructing pay brackets and for career progression of individuals. It has been found of practical convenience, therefore, to subdivide the work-strata into grades, each grade within each work-stratum being expressed in time-span of discretion. These grades are not for managerial organization; a person may be upgraded through all the grades in a stratum without having to change in organizational position, and a manager may have subordinates in any or all of the grades in the next lower stratum.

Thus, for example, Stratum II, running form 3-months to 1-year time-span, can be subdivided by fixing grading boundaries at 6-months and 9-months time-span, giving grades IIC, IIB and IIA as shown:

```
           ┌ ────────1 Year ──────────────────────────────
           │                        Grade IIA
           │      _____9 months  _____
Stratum II │                        Grade IIB
           │      _____6 months  _____
           │                        Grade IIC
           └ _____ 3 months _____
```

The way in which this system of work-strata and grades can be used to establish a flexible and workable differential incomes policy will be described in Chapter 8.

The Differential Concertina

The material from the foregoing three chapters can now be put together into a method for stating a complete differential wage and salary payment structure for all employees at all levels of work throughout a whole nation, or for each main region of very large nations that may have major regional differences.

It should be recalled that wage and salary payment refers to the total value in wage or salary in monetary terms of a person's total emolument for whatever is the contractually established normal work-week. It comprises the sum of actual wage and salary plus the equivalent value in wage or salary of all special benefits such as provision of a car, special insurances, stock options, which are given in lieu of money as an identifiable part of wage and salary.

Those to Whom These Differential Figures Do not Apply

It is important to note that these differential payment figures refer only to total emolument expressed in wages and salaries of those engaged as employees, on employment contracts, in true employment systems, right up to and including the highest-level salaried executives. It is just as important to be clear about those to whom these figures do not apply.

The equitable differential payment scale does not apply to: private business owners; self-employed professionals, including doctors, lawyers, architects, engineers, and other professionals in private practice; university teaching staff—they are on special tenured part-time contracts; clergy—they are, in England, on special stipendiary forms of reward; self-employed technicians and skilled workers, such as plumbers, electricians, repairmen, decorators in business on their own; musicians, actors, singers, sculptors, painters, and other self-employed artists; and finally, those who derive their incomes from rents and from return on investments.

The Equitable Differential Work-Payment Structure

The norms of felt-fair payment for given levels of work measured in time-span in any given nation or region can be stated in terms of the structure of work-strata and grading described in the last chapter. What happens when this step is taken is shown in the accompanying table of the emolument levels that were expressed as equitable by those at the various levels, in the United States and in England in June 1980. The monetary values will have changed in level by the time this statement is read, depending upon the rate of earnings inflation in the two countries.

The table does not, of course, set out what the actual levels of pay for given levels of work were in the United States and in England in June 1980, but only what people felt would have been differentially fair. The actual pay distribution in the United States tended in general to follow the equitable pattern, whereas in England actual pay was markedly compressed at the very bottom and at the upper-middle and higher levels as compared with felt-fair pay—a fact which was widely identified and experienced as a pay compression and inequity at the bottom and at the top. Moreover, there was a much greater dispersion of the actual pay levels of individuals than there was for felt-fair pay. (See Figure 9.1.)

The practical question, however, is not what is the equitable distribution of pay at any given time—that can be established by taking soundings of felt-fair pay related to measured time-spans. It is rather the question of what should be the general level of wages and salaries at any given time, what should be the differential distribution of those wages and salaries, and how they should be decided and by whom. To answer these questions, a method of putting pay policies in the form of what may be termed a differential concertina will be described.

The Differential Concertina
To establish a systematic policy for wages and salaries is a twofold problem. The first problem is that of what the general levels should be this year compared, say, with last year. Should increases in general be kept, say, to 3 percent, or 6 percent, or 12 percent, or, indeed, should there be any increases at all?

The second problem is that of whether any adjustment of differentials is called for. Has the pay structure become too compressed, for example, so that there might be more latitude for relatively greater percentage increases in the higher salary ranges? Or is it considered that the lowest-paid workers are so badly off relative to everyone else that the bottom end of the pay scale should be brought up differentially not only in relation to the middle and higher levels but in relation also even to those just above them at the lower levels?

The first problem is somewhat easier to take care of than the second; it is a simple matter at least to state a policy, even though it may

Time-Span Level Base Line	Stratum	Grade	Felt-Fair Wage and Salary Levels - 1980	
			U.S. $	England £
	VII			
30 Years			510,000	
		C		
20 YEARS			430,000	
		A		
17 Years			350,000	
	VI	B		
13 Years			285,000	
		C		
10 YEARS			215,000	70,000
		A		
8 Years			170,000	56,000
	V	B		
6½ Years			140,000	45,000
		C		
5 YEARS			118,000	35,000
		A		
4 Years			91,000	30,000
	IV	B		
3 Years			75,000	24,000
		C		
2 YEARS			60,000	19,500
		A		
20 Months			49,000	16,000
	III	B		
16 Months			40,000	14,000
		C		
1 YEAR			32,500	10,500
		A		
9 Months			28,000	9,000
	II	B		
6 Months			24,000	8,000
		C		
3 MONTHS			20,500	7,000
		A		
1 Month			17,500	5,800
	I	B		
1 Week			14,000	4,700
		C		
1 Day			12,000	4,000
		D		

Figure 8.1. Equitable wage and salary levels in the United States and England in June 1980.

be politically explosive to implement it, especially if actual differentials
are out of line with equitable differentials. The second problem, however, that of getting the differential structure right, has so far proven
intractable; for there has not as yet been any means even of stating
policies, let alone agreeing on them.

If the problem of wage and salary levels and differentials is to be
solved, a mechanism is required which will make it possible to express
both the general level of wages and salaries and the total pattern of
differentials in one single policy statement. Such a policy statement can
be made in terms of a generalization of the structure of work-strata and
grades described, as shown in Figure 8.2, in the form of a differential
concertina.

In Figure 8.2, a series of different possible policies is illustrated.
None of these, of course, is an actual policy. But what can be shown is
how the differential concertina can be changed in shape: it can be
compressed or expanded as a whole; or it can be compressed at either
end (or in the middle) and held constant at the other end. And it can be
changed in level as a whole, or it can be changed both in level and in
shape.

The significance of a wage and salary policy stated in terms of the
differential concertina is that it gives the same payment brackets for all
jobs which fall into any given level-of-work brackets, or grades. Any
two jobs, for example, whose measured time-spans fall between 6
months and 9 months would be graded IIB and acquire the pay brackets
currently applying to that grade; the occupants of such roles would be
paid within that payment bracket. By this means everyone working in a
job in the same grade would be paid within the same pay bracket,
regardless of occupation, regardless of locality, of dirt, danger, or
discomfort, of race, sex, or color, of the training which was required to
get the job, of length of service, and regardless of anything else—a
basis for differential reward which was shown in Chapter 6 to be what
people universally experience as just and fair.

If a job remained relatively constant in level of work, so would the
grade and the relative payment level. If it increased or decreased in
level, it would pick up its appropriate grade. The absolute levels of
these differential payment brackets, and their relationship to profit
levels, entrepreneurial and rent and investment incomes, and levels of
government expenditure, will be considered in Chapter 9.

Recognition of Individual Performance
The equitable differential work—payment structure sets the wage and
salary bracket for each and every employment role. Each role picks up

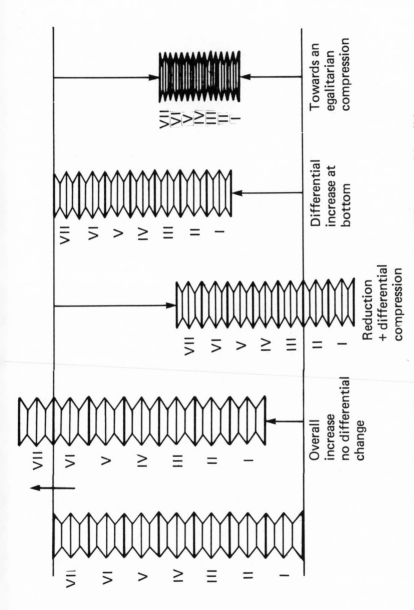

Figure 8.2. The differential concertina, with examples of different possible policies.

the payment bracket of the grade into which it falls by virtue of its measured time-span. Two questions then arise: where in that payment bracket does an individual fall? and how does an individual move from one bracket to a higher (or lower) bracket?

The first of these questions—that of a person's position in a payment bracket—can be answered in many ways. It can be subject to automatic progression through the bracket at an agreed annual rate. It can be subject to managerial assessment of performance and merit review, or subject, if desired, to peer-group assessment.

The question of upgrading and promotion (movement up to the next higher work-stratum) must be a matter of managerial decision. It must be decided, first, whether there is available work in the enterprise to allow of upgrading or promotion; and second, whether a particular individual warrants such upgrading or promotion. It is likely that individuals will seek progression in level of work, and consequently in payment, at a rate that coincides with the rate of maturation of their level of capability.[1] The final safeguard for the individual against underrecognition and underemployment must be the general availability of abundant employment in the community. Abundant employment enables people to seek, and to find, their own proper level in employment.

At the same time it must also be recognized that availability of abundant employment can readily undermine adequate discipline in employment systems. The appropriate counterbalancing forces for indiscipline are rewards and advancement related to performance appraisal. It is in this regard that the idea of individual position in pay brackets being determined by peer-group rating has merit: in a setting of mutual trust a peer group has little sympathy with any of its members who try to corrupt the situation.

Setting the Differential Concertina

The construction of the differential concertina radically simplifies the problem of stating a practical policy for wage and salary differentials. The setting of differentials may present a difficult political problem; but the concertina overcomes the technical difficulties of stating what the differential pattern might be. The possibilities range all the way from a purely egalitarian distribution (that is to say, all employees receive the same emolument regardless of level of work) to a very wide distribution

---

[1] The evidence for this proposition, and for systematic career progression, is described in Elliott Jaques, (1961), *Equitable Payment,* Chapters 9 and 10; and (1968), *Progression Handbook.*

of the type characterized by the U.S. distribution illustrated in Figure 8.1, or the even more open distributions in some socialist countries when fringe benefits such as apartments and country residences, cars and chauffeurs, special shopping facilities, are taken into account.

It will be evident that the level and differential pattern of wages and salaries must apply to all employment roles at all levels, and throughout a whole nation or politically separate region. There can be no room for local variations, or for variations in individual enterprises, even with agreement between employers and employees. If employers wish to pay above equity in order to attract people, they should not be allowed to do so; for they would be introducing local differential instability into the surrounding geographical area and into the area of business of which they are a part. And if employees wish to agree to accept differentially lower wages and salaries as a permanent arrangement, they should not be allowed to do so; they should take all their earnings but, if they so wish, reinvest part of them in the business, becoming shareholders as any other investor would do; they should not introduce a local lowering of rates of pay.

There are all kinds of arguments put forward for having local or regional variations in wage and salary levels. But the arguments are mutually contradictory. Thus, because transport costs are higher from outlying districts to the metropolitan area, the pay in outlying districts should be lower if there is to be adequate investment in those areas; but rents and rates and services are cheaper in outlying districts, therefore labor costs do not need to be lowered. Or, people in country districts have to pay more for travel, entertainment, and amenities than people in urban areas, and should therefore be differentially favored in pay; but it is more expensive to live in urban areas, and people in country districts have the advantages of living in the healthy countryside, with cheap fresh food, therefore pay in urban areas should be higher. For every argument there is a counterargument. That is why differential pay levels should be the same everywhere; people can then choose where they wish to live; industry can also choose where it goes to find its labor force; geographical imbalances in industrial investment should be tackled by investment policies and locating sovereign services, and not by manipulations of the differential wage and salary structure.

With policies set by the differential concertina, the level of wages and salaries and the pattern of differentials become a national issue to be settled nationally. And so they ought to be. What an industrial nation as a whole can afford to disburse within itself in the form of wages and salaries is a matter of the most profound socioeconomic importance.

Wage and salary differentials would no longer be left to be settled by coercive bargaining by leapfrogging groups of employers and employees. The question for entrepreneurial employers should be to determine how many people they should employ, and what levels of work to establish in order to get their work done, so as to run a profitable business at the going rates of pay, a business whose profitability is based upon the attractiveness of the goods and services it can offer to the market and not upon how clever the employers are in bargaining down the rates of pay of their employees.

It is the responsible legislature which should decide the level and shape of the differential concertina, by at least an annual review. It is through the legislative process alone that a people as a whole can decide on an equitable distribution of wages and salaries and their general level. Such actions do not constitute unnecessary government intrusion into personal freedom. By the policy described, the earnings of freely competitive entrepreneurs are left free from government intervention. But individual wages and salaries never have been free, nor can they be. It is the whole force of my argument and data that wage and salary differentials are structurally locked into the differential structure of the level of work in employment hierarchies; they are not, nor can they ever be, determined by the free play of supply and demand among freely acting individual producers and consumers operating under the exigencies of day-to-day oscillations in an open market.

The time is long overdue for open argument, and statement of cases, of the reasons for maintaining any particular distribution of wage and salary income differentials in industrialized employment societies—for debate of the whole structure, and not just the structure for the manual and clerical worker majority. To let the issue go by default, to pretend not to notice it and to look the other way, is to deepen suspicion and mistrust about who is getting away with what.

It is in order to dispel the miasma of cunning secretiveness and distrust that open rational discussion of differentials is so important. Let a nation face openly the standard of living it can afford. Equally, let it face in open argument and debate, by ordinary democratic process, the relative distribution of that standard of living which it believes is right and proper, fair and just, and realistic in rewarding differential levels of contribution in work for the common weal. The equitable differential wage and salary concertina provides the mechanism which makes this open rational debate possible. It is this openness of debate which can be a major contribution to the good society; politically debated agreement on differentials can be just and fair and can confer freedom. It is the coercive and secretive approach which is unjust; while seeming to leave people free to get what they want, it in fact reduces freedom by rewarding coercion—and it breeds violence in society.

PART FOUR

POLITICAL ECONOMY AND THE GOOD SOCIETY

CHAPTER 9

Political Settlement of Wage and Salary Levels

The reason that unemployment has had to be used as an economic regulator lies in the inability to prevent wage and salary levels from running away under the impact of coercive bargaining once an economy begins to heat up—that is to say, as soon as an industrial nation begins to be threatened by economic success. In this chapter I shall show how it is possible to deal with the general level of wages and salaries in relation to other key factors in the economy, such as profit levels, investment, government spending, and pensions, and with the differential distribution of wages and salaries. This will be done in such a way as to make it possible to sustain employment at a level of abundance which produces all-round gratification and national unity and goodwill; with free enterprise that is a national asset because it is constructively competitive and released from the guilt-inducing institutionally driven exploitation of employees; and with a firmly established and assured economic equity.

In the following chapter an additional subject will be introduced. It is that of the need, once an employment society has become established, to counterpoint the establishment of nationwide equitable wage and salary levels and of abundant employment, by the assurance locally of opportunity for full employee participation; this means employee participation in the development of policy within each enterprise in connection with the impact of those policies upon employment conditions and opportunities. In this issue is to be found the twentieth-century equivalent of the extension of the political franchise during the nineteenth century.

Finally, the argument would not be complete without examining the interwoven question of equality of opportunity. Equal opportunity is commonly confused with egalitarianism in level of income. They are most decidedly not the same. Equal opportunity is an axiomatic human right. By contrast, the actual distribution of socioeconomic status is a politically debatable subject; and in any case equal economic status cannot be legislated, since no one can control the use which individuals and families make of their resources.

The last chapter will be concerned with the contribution which the assurance of abundant employment, wage and salary equity, and free enterprise can make to the achievement of equality of opportunity. Brief consideration will be given to the closely related subjects of the position of inheritance and of what would constitute a reasonable workweek to which people would be entitled, in a truly equal-opportunity society.

Actual Wage and Salary Distributions

The first problem to be resolved is that of the practicality of the politics of getting a national openly agreed settlement of wage and salary levels and differentials by due democratic governmental process, not only without weakening freedom of enterprise but strengthening it in the process. Some of the difficulties involved can be illustrated by reference to the actual pay levels in the United States and England.

It should be noted that the comparisons between the two countries can be made only because it is possible to compare the pay relativities in terms of common levels of work measured in time-span. That is to say, the differential concertinas for both the felt-fair wage and salary distributions and the actual wage and salary distributions can be compared directly, regardless of differences in currency or of changes in the rate of exchange. In short, the differential concertina makes it possible to compare directly, between one nation and any other, the pattern of distribution of socioeconomic status provided by wages and salaries.

In Figure 9.1 will be seen a rough approximation to the actual situation in the United States and England, based on data collected between July and September 1979. It may be noted that the pattern of felt-fair pay is practically identical for the two countries. There is effectively a doubling of felt-fair pay for each work-stratum.[1] The pattern of actual payment, however, differs considerably between the countries.

In the United States the actual pay distribution is not far off the distribution that would be consistent with felt-fair pay. In England there is a greater discrepancy between felt-fair and actual pay, as a result of a falling away of actual pay from felt-fair pay from Stratum III upward. This deviation between actual pay and felt-fair pay is the consequence of a succession of freezes on increases in medium and high salaries

---

[1] A possible explanation for this doubling of felt-fair pay for each addition of one work-stratum, in terms of the Weber-Fechner law in psychology, will be found in Elliott Jaques, (1976), *A General Theory of Bureaucracy*, p. 135 fn.

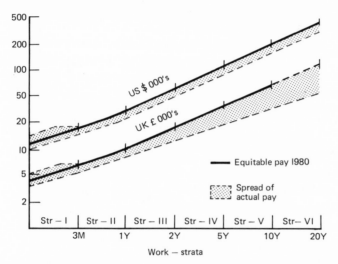

Figure 9.1. The equitable (felt-fair) work-payment scale for the United States and England, and the relationship between the felt-fair pay levels and the approximate distribution of actual pay levels for the two countries.

between 1973 and 1979. These differences can be seen by comparing the two distributions in Figure 9.1.

The question is whether either of these actual distributions can be said to be politically right or wrong. It is not possible to answer this question, because both the level and the pattern of wages and salaries have not been debated as such in either of these countries, nor in any other country. These levels and distributions have happened as a result of a combination of political and coercive forces: coercive bargaining and what particular industries have felt they could afford; attitudes toward what the pay scales should be in various areas of public employment—government, health, education, welfare, the armed forces, nationalized industries; regional variations and the availability of immigrant labor; reactions to "brain drain"; governmental pay freezes, and special actions such as the freezing of higher-level salaries; the imposition of productivity bargaining policies; the actions of arbitration and conciliation systems; variations in the strength of union organization in different industries and in different geographical areas.

Underneath all these manifest forces which are well recognized as the forces of an imperfect labor market, there lie the unrecognized forces of felt differential equity and inequity. It is these forces that lead to feelings in the various countries about the nature of the distribution. There are feelings, for example, that there is a compression of salaries at the middle and the top not only in England, but also in Canada.

There are also feelings between particular sectors within these countries; for example, it is felt that the so-called semiskilled occupations are unfairly overtaking the skilled trades in pay. Feelings like these—and they have very substantial effects upon political outlooks and industrial relations—cannot be explained in market terms, nor do they simply go away in the face of market forces.

What then should the levels and the distribution be? Let us turn to the issues which have to be taken into account if the differential concertina is to be used for settling these questions.

Differential Distribution of Wages and Salaries

The problem of the general level of wages and salaries—that is to say, the total amount to be paid—must be settled year by year in relation to the other prime factors in a national economy. If that total amount is to be debated and set in a reasonable and acceptable way, the pattern of differential distribution of that amount must have been clearly debated and settled in its own right in terms of the prevailing norms of equity. What the outcome of such debates would be, however, it is not as yet possible to foresee, since the politics of differentials are shrouded in doubt and uncertainty.

To start with what is clear, it is not possible to proceed with a sound and complete wage and salary policy unless differentials are included. It is not even possible to debate the issue intelligently or effectively. If wage and salary levels are to go up, or to go down, or to stay the same, individuals want to know, and are entitled to know, how their own individual circumstances will be affected: "What will happen to my pay?" is the direct question. "Will we all go up, or come down, at the same rate? And if so, should the same rate mean the same percentage increase or decrease, or should it mean the same absolute money value? Or will some of us stay where we are, while others go up or down? Or will some of us go up and others down, while the overall total remains the same?" These are the kinds of issues that have to be faced. General overall levels are simply not discussable in any reasonable manner unless people can be put in a position to understand how the outcome of the debate will affect them personally; without this personal link the debate cannot become grounded in social reality.

Moreover, when, as regularly occurs, general levels of wages and salaries are discussed in the absence of any reference to differentials and to the full impact on everyone, anxiety and suspicion are generated because the crux of the argument—namely, who gets what as compared with whom—is obscured. The question of who is to gain most in times of prosperity, and who is to suffer most in times of adversity, cannot be allowed to go by default if the members of a nation are to be enabled to live and to work together, to have confidence in one another, and to face squarely their economic reality and agree on what to do about it.

With the degree of uncertainty and mutual watchfulness that exists, it is not to be wondered at that movement in wage and salary levels is sticky downward, as the economists say. With no explicit mechanisms that are likely to prove fair and just in application, the only reasonable thing to do is to hang on to whatever gains have been made, and to await the chance to leap forward again relative to others. There is certainly no leeway for giving anything away.

It is difficult to predict what arguments people are likely to bring forward if and when a serious public debate about differentials is undertaken under proper constitutional conditions. What would the debate sound like in the United States, say, or in the United Kingdom? Are their distributions too flat or too steep, or are they each perhaps right for the social, political, and economic circumstances in these nations at this time, or should either nation perhaps have a flatter or a steeper distribution? The problem is that there are no established principles on which to argue these issues of who should get how much as compared with whom.

What is needed is to develop such principles for settling the pay relativities. Perhaps (as would be my hunch) they will turn out to be consistent with the equitable wage and salary distributions which have been discovered so far. Perhaps they will tend toward egalitarianism. Perhaps they will be different for different nations and for the same nation at different times. But whatever the principles to be elaborated, it is essential to recognize the need to have them, and to continue no longer with the confusion and uncertainty and social fragmentation of the present coercive power methods which offer so much scope to the manipulators and to the heavy brigades.

The basic issue is how much trust we are willing to put into the arena of constitutional practice; or how much we fear that in the area of pay relativities, which is so politically sensitive and suffused with so much self-seeking and greed, there is no chance for due governmental process to work. The differential concertina, by making this open and public debate possible, can force everyone to make up their minds about their belief in the efficacy of due democratic process.

Minimum Pay Levels

I have said that there are no established principles for settling by legitimate political means what a fair and just general distribution of pay differentials would be in a nation as a whole. To the best of my knowledge no nation has ever openly debated the issue. There is, however, one issue which is likely to be pressed forward and to demand attention as the first issue to be resolved. That issue is the question of what the minimum wage and salary level should be—the level upon which the whole of the differential concertina would stand.

Given an abundant employment society, I cannot see that due public debate could do other than set a reasonable minimum pay level that would eliminate true poverty. No self-respecting society could do otherwise. It is only when poverty occurs by default—as a result of seemingly powerful economic or even psychological forces outside the control of man—that people can tolerate the existence of poverty on their own doorstep and hold their consciences at bay.

I am assuming here that the special problems of the handicapped and disabled, and of temporarily or permanently unemployable persons, would be taken care of by social means. Although I am not considering these social issues here, I would have no doubt that a society that is suffused with a feeling of equity and justice in differential economic rewards would ensure adequate care of those who were not able fully to look after themselves. Equity in pay is a powerful diffuser of all-round fairness. The setting of a reasonable foundation wage could be such as to underwrite maximum freedom of choice for everyone—the effect that is sought, for example, by the proponents of negative income tax. It would continually ensure as strong a home market as the world economy would allow, as an economic basis for a thrusting and consumer-oriented free enterprise.

The General Level of Wages and Salaries

Once abundant employment has been assured, and the pattern of differential distribution of wages and salaries has been agreed, the next problem to be settled by government and a legislature attempting to determine a wage and salary policy is what ought to be the total amount to be distributed in this form. It is the politically explosive decision about how much the people of a nation can afford to distribute to themselves via the employment sector in wages and salaries, as compared with the total sum distributed in profits, in dividends, in pensions, and in government expenditures. Upon this decision rests the standard of living to be enjoyed for the ensuing period by those who work as employees. It is with respect to this issue—as against differentials—that wages and salaries must be treated as part of the control system of the economy of a nation, to be taken into account along with all the other macroeconomic factors.

Here the prime questions are of the following kind: Can the nation afford a real increase in standard of living? If so, how much—1 percent or 2 percent, 3 percent or 4½ percent, or —? Have import prices gone up so that a 1½ percent, or a 6 percent, or whatever, increase is required in order to maintain the standard of living? Or is the economic situation such that no increase can be given and a slight erosion of standard of living is the best that can be expected if damaging inflation is to be avoided? Or has there been a drive on capital investment to increase the numbers of jobs available and reduce unemployment, thus necessitating some moderation of consumer spending so as to avoid internal inflation and an excessive demand for imports?

Questions such as these cannot be settled on their own. They must be debated in relation to the levels of profits being earned, the amounts being earned from rents and investments, and the amounts being spent on governmentally provided goods and services. Increases and decreases in the total wage and salary income sector will have substantial effects upon the amounts in these other sectors. What these relationships should be, which sectors should be given additional encouragement at any given time, are matters of high public policy.

It is out of this open and public debate that the people of a nation can become aware of what they can really afford in the sense of the standard of living to which they are entitled by virtue of the natural resources, their level of investment, their productivity from their technology and capital equipment, and their work. They can be faced squarely, for example, with the consequences of national borrowing (if they should decide that they want to have more than they can afford). And they can encounter, in terms directly connected with the reality of their own wage and salary expectations, the meaning of various levels of investment in future prospects as against immediate gratification whatever the consequences for the future.

Macroeconomic issues, such as the relation between the general level of wages and salaries, profits, employment, and productivity, can be brought sharply down to earth when a nation is offered the opportunity to decide what it shall take for itself in wages and salaries as a practical matter in relation to these other and connected factors. Thus, for example, once the differential distribution of wages and salaries has been agreed to, people can turn to that other major differential, that between the total amount to be distributed in profits and the total in wages and salaries. This differential is part of the macroeconomic debate on the best ways to maintain a sound national economy. This macroeconomic debate can be pursued much more effectively once it has been extricated from the emotional microeconomics of where each individual wage and salary earner will be in the pecking order.

People can be asked to examine and to take account of such major issues as: the effects of labor costs on prices and on international competitiveness and the ability to import; the consequences for employment and national wealth of steps calculated to reduce or to increase the sum total of profits and so to encourage or discourage entrepreneurial risk and activity. They will be able to do so in a much more realistic and constructive frame of mind so long as they are not dragged down by anxieties about employment and suspicions about what others might be up to in order to gain unfair differential advantages.

In short, so long as there is no way of ensuring abundant employment and of achieving an equitable differential distribution of wages and salaries that can be perceived to be equitable, the macroeconomic debate, which includes the total amount of wages and salaries to be distributed, cannot take place in sound and practical terms. The moment, however, a mechanism is established for stating and agreeing upon the differential distribution, and for permanently establishing abundant employment, the macroeconomic debate can be effectively pursued, and can include the question of the total amount to be paid in wages and salaries as against other competing rights and demands.

The Rights of Minorities

But how likely is it, it may be asked, that a nation will preserve what people at higher levels might regard as reasonable differentials? Would not the majority, who are at the lower end of the concertina, vote to abolish differentials altogether, or at least to bring about a mighty compression of the differential concertina? If such a decision were to come about, it would at least do so by due democratic process of open persuasive debate in a legislature. But in fact such a dramatic change would not take place: for the play of coercive power would already have brought it about.

But more important is the fact that this problem is in no way new. It is the old and absolutely fundamental problem of the democratic process, namely, how are the rights of minorities to be catered for? The democratic process is based not simply upon the will of the majority but also upon the continued good-hearted participation of the various minorities. The democratic process assumes the existence of general values and norms in society which encompass the needs of minorities as well as of the majority, and which representative argument and debate can express. It is these values which must be reflected in the decisions taken. The equitable pay differentials are an explicit example of such values. The fact that they are now made explicit by the differential concertina may give a new dimension to democratic debate.

Wage and Salary Incomes and Profits

It has been indicated that if general profit levels are deemed to be getting out of line with the general level of incomes, whatever the political and economic grounds for believing so, that relationship can be readily changed: first by adjusting the total amount to be distributed in wage and salary incomes; and second by adjusting taxation on corporate or self-employed profits.

The macroeconomic relationship between the general levels of wage and salary incomes and of personal and corporate profitability is influenced by the levels of wages and salaries, for those levels have a substantial effect upon profitability. Thus, if wage and salary levels are given a real increase and the standard of living of the employee sector is increased, then opportunities for better profitability are enhanced. And contrariwise, decreases in employee standard of living will most certainly decrease the general levels of profitability. It is within these general policy limits that profitability must be allowed to run free.

But what about the profits of individual private enterprises, personal or corporate? Should there not be some sharing of profits by employees? Profit-sharing at the microeconomic level is often supposed to be an incentive to employees, a matter of reward for the special effort which has created the profits. But that view would be difficult to uphold in the long term. Such payments obfuscate equitable differential pay structures. It is better to leave those employees who wish to share in profits to do so by shareholding: and to concentrate their working efforts on gaining full employment of their talents and equitable pay for that work.

To implement profit-sharing for employees has all the drawbacks of bonus incentive schemes, including piecework bonuses and productivity bonuses. They confuse output with individual performance. I have already indicated how good performance must be recognized: an individual is to be rewarded by progress in individual earnings and in due progress in regard to the level of work. Given these conditions, any individual who is doing a reasonable day's work will be receiving a differentially reasonable day's pay and reasonable progression. That is what fair pay is about.

Corporate profitability, after payment of the cost of money in dividends for the use of shareholders' capital, and other charges for money capital, and the cost of labor, should go into replenishment of equipment and into development, and into the attraction of further capital. It helps to create jobs. Corporate profits compete with wage and salary incomes. Any abuses and improper use of profits have to be dealt with in their own right: they are not corrected by profit-sharing.

Profitability has to do with the financial situation *after* all employees, at all levels, have been duly and properly rewarded. It is a function of economic production methods, of successful new products and services, of sound and competitive pricing and marketing, and of wise business policies. That is why it is just and fair that corporate profits should be used for the development of the enterprise and for employment security and job creation. It is always open to employees to choose to become shareholders by investing, and to take their due risk in sharing in profitability or loss.

Personal profitability of those who run personal private enterprises may seem different from corporate profitability. For the true private entrepreneurs do gain personally from the profits. Indeed, they may choose how to dispose of the profits by apportionment to private income or to personal gain by further investment in the business. The catch, of course, is that there may or may not be any profits. Private entrepreneurs risk having no income: the counterbalancing factor is the opportunity to gain large incomes if they possess the socially important ability to understand and to foresee consumer needs, and if their efforts to satisfy those needs are particularly successful.

Personal private enterprise is based upon private personal risk of gain or loss. That is a delicately balanced issue. It is not to be interfered with, or related to wage- and salary-earning levels, other than in the most general way; it is related, that is, at the macroeconomic level in terms of the total amount paid in wages and salaries, and the total amount of earned profit. Private company taxation is a proper charge upon a private company; once that charge has been made and paid, entrepreneurs should be left to get on with taking the best care they can of their personal risk. They are the source of much personalized service and sensitive provision of special goods, and a rich source of creation of new types of useful enterprise and accompanying new types of employment.

In short, it is abundant employment and an equitable differential wage and salary distribution which guarantee the earnings rights of all employees to which all employers must conform. Within this context, no employing enterprise can exploit its employees on pay; that position having been secured, entrepreneurs should be encouraged, for the good of society, to pursue their entrepreneurial activities.

Relation to Cost of Living and to Social Benefits

The cost of living is one of many factors to be taken into account by the legislators who debate and determine the wage and salary levels and differentials. But there is an insidious tendency these days to try to get pay and pensions linked to changes in the cost of living—or at least to increases in the cost of living, for no one likes to agree to a reduction in standard of living. Such cost-of-living indexation is an open cheque, a guarantee to maintain the standard of living of a group or of a whole nation. But no enterprise or nation can give such a guarantee. Whether or not a given standard of living can be maintained or increased is a matter of whether or not the level of output and trade makes it possible.

The procedure outlined not only makes it possible for a nation explicitly to decide and to keep under review the standard of living it can afford to distribute; it makes it mandatory that this review should take place at least annually and be publicly debated and determined. Payments such as pensions can then be indexed if need be; but they should be indexed not in relation to the cost-of-living index but to the earnings index. That is to say, changes in pension levels should be kept in line with changes in the general levels of wages and salaries. By this means, pensioners and recipients of similar social benefits would receive a standard of living which would vary in the same way as that of all other wage and salary earners, with no special guarantee of any given standard of living being maintained. The whole conception is that of one nation experiencing equivalent increases or decreases in standard of living, sharing equitably in prosperity and depression, where what is equitable is what is publicly and openly determined by due democratic political process to be an equitable differential distribution.

Special Payments and Safeguards against Employer-Employee Collusion

It might well be that some employers and employees would try to collude for their own purposes in order to subvert the system. An employer, for example, who desired to attract particular types of employee who were in short supply might want secretly to offer pay levels above the national policy, and the rest of the employees would tacitly agree to say nothing in the hope that their turn to get the same advantage might come one day. Or employers might get their employees to drop their rates pro tem to help the firm over a lean period, and then leave the rates depressed thereafter so as to exploit, say, an immigrant population. As indicated, such collusive disregard of national policy should be prevented. It could be prevented without too much difficulty.

Part of the problem of keeping control arises from the fact that there may be circumstances in which special payments should be made to employees over and above their wages and salaries, especially in connection with the problem of labor mobility mentioned in Chapter 4. Such circumstances would include: moving expenses for changing jobs from one locality to another; specially authorized payments to encourage employees to move to localities in which there is a scarcity of people with the skills and qualities necessary to maintain local work or to contribute to growing and developing enterprises.

Any such special payments must be paid as lump sums, or as some kind of spread-out increment, but *not*—and this point is of great importance—built into the wage and salary. The differential wage and salary structure must be maintained in clear relationship to levels of work. Thus, to take an extreme example, suppose it were agreed to be essential to pay a special increment to persuade a highly skilled technologist working at Grade IIIB level to switch to a high-priority enterprise. He might be offered, say, 30 percent above the appropriate differential pay level for the Grade IIIB role. But the work would still be designated IIIB, not IIIA or IVC; his salary bracket would be the IIIB salary bracket; and he would be shown to be receiving a 30 percent scarcity increment separate from his wage or salary, this increment to be allowed to be eroded away as and when the scarcity existed no more.

Allowing for special payments of this kind suggests that it might be possible for employers and employees to collude to pay wages and salaries outside the national policy. They might do this, for example, by placing roles in higher grades than were warranted by their time-span measurements; or perhaps by pushing everyone to the top of their payment grade. Any such collusion could be monitored and controlled readily.

Collusion would be difficult to maintain in large enterprises. It would have to be collusion on such a massive scale that it would readily become known in the community. The collusion could not be carried out in limited sectors of such enterprises because it would throw the manifest differential payment structure out of balance and would be objected to by at least some individuals in other sectors. Employee representatives, as described in Chapter 10, would have a substantial role to play in this regard.

Even the monitoring of small enterprises would not be too difficult. The collusive practices would show up at the boundaries of work-strata. Thus, too many skilled manual roles would show up in Stratum II, too many professional roles in Stratum III, and so on. And if everyone were paid at the top of their bracket, that would show up in a crowding of the pay distribution against the top line of each bracket.

The objection will inevitably be raised that the measurement of time-span and the control of collusion that are called for would lead to the creation of an army of specialists and government officials. The exact opposite is the case. An army of specialists already exists in every industrial country today; it would be decreased by the procedures outlined. These specialists presently comprise: work-study, personnel, and job evaluation experts engaged in the wasteful activity of evaluating work by unrealistic methods; and the personnel and industrial relations experts, the trade union leaders and other employee representatives, the managers, and the officials from arbitration and conciliation offices, who are engaged year in and year out in the endlessly repeating rounds of negotiations which are always and inevitably inconclusive. Far fewer staff would be required to administer work measurement and pay within a nationally established and comprehensive differential concertina: and the product of their work would be more realistic and manageable employment systems and an objective understanding of the work in those systems.

The Problem of Inflation

Finally, we may turn to the problem of inflation. Our analysis and the policies stemming from that analysis have radically altered the problem in three ways: first, the elements of inflation due to wage−push and salary−push leapfrogging have been eliminated; second, the problem of dealing with inflation has been untied from the problems of maintaining abundant employment and of dealing with wage and salary differentials; and third, the problem of wage and salary inflation has been separated completely from prices of goods and services. The consequences are considerable.

The control of inflation, while remaining a complex problem, would nevertheless be less complex because the cost−push forces causing inflation would have been eliminated as an uncontrollable factor. The control of inflation would be both technically and politically simplified. It would not be necessary to take into account the incalculable and unpredictable effects which any given economic policies might have upon demands for increases in wages and salaries, with their interactive feeding back into the inflationary pressures. And it would not be necessary to impose price controls, and thus ruin the free commodity market mechanisms, as a sop for getting wage and salary controls accepted.

A nation that could thus attend to inflation, without anxiety about unemployment or about differential pay, and without having to hobble freedom of enterprise and the free play of commodity market competition, would be a nation that could argue rationally about the causes of inflation and about what ought to be done. Moreover, it could remain a united nation while doing so, because it would not be internally torn by people fighting one another for work in short supply or for differential advantages in pay.

Under these conditions, policy-makers and economists could have a proper job to do, in assessing the likely GNP for the year ahead, and then deciding whether personal incomes should increase or decrease. The control of inflation and of standard of living in these circumstances would not necessarily be easy. But it would not be the seemingly impossible task that it has become in these days of stagflation. And it would not be bedeviled by having to choose between full employment and inflation on the one hand and unemployment and deflation on the other. It would come into perspective as a political economic problem to be solved by normal political means, in a setting of assured abundance of employment, assured equity pay, and full freedom of competitive enterprise.

These views may be thought to be unrealistically idealistic and utopian. They are not. Requisite constitutional procedures, procedures which are experienced as open, fair, and just, become highly valued. Corruption and violence thrive where freedom and justice do not exist, or cannot patently be seen to exist and to be participated in. Good institutions, and the sense of freedom they generate, breed an enormously protective attitude toward them. People really do value institutions which support and enshrine freedom and justice. They are unlikely to stand by and see them dissipated by corrupt collusion. It is not an accident that the ideas of freedom and justice have the same linguistic metaphoric root as the ideas of truth and trust and faith—they all generate and reinforce one another.

CHAPTER 10

Coercion and Participation

Effective management of the employment sector is one of the critical areas for industrial nations. We have so far considered only the political economic context of management—the free enterprise market, equitable pay differentials, and abundant employment, which are some of the main conditions and constraints within which employment systems might most effectively operate. There are many other conditions, however, which must be achieved within employment systems if they are to contribute to economic prosperity with freedom and justice. One such condition, which is closely related to the issue of coercive power in wage and salary negotiation, is effective provision for employee participation in policy-making. Such arrangements are needed to cope in a constitutional manner with the power relationship between employers and employees in such a way as to legitimate it and transform it into authority from which all can gain, rather than to absorb it, as at present, into institutions organized for mutual coercion by which in the end everyone must lose.

There are two significant reasons in the present context for considering employee participation in policy-making. One reason is that all policies inevitably affect the employment and career opportunities within the employment system of any enterprise—and hence are linked to the availability of abundant employment for employees. The second reason is that the issue of employee participation is the counterpart, inside employment systems, of wage and salary negotiations in the wider social field in which the employment systems are embedded. The substitution of employee participation for mutual employer–employee coercion may be a necessary condition for the confidence which will be needed for any switch to a requisite wage and salary policy and the relinquishing of coercive power bargaining.

Adequate participation in policy-making is especially important for dealing constructively with changes in any enterprise which may reduce the numbers of people employed—whether changes in markets and sales, or in methods or organization. Any such contractions or closures should be subject to consideration by the employees who have invested their work in the enterprise and whose immediate careers are at stake. The existence of a surrounding abundant employment environment would make it possible for employee participation to be freed from the massive anxiety and insecurity which has always attended the possibility of unemployment.

Open Management

A case has been made for more openness in society in setting wage and salary levels and differentials, as against closed secrecy. Openness expresses trust and trustworthiness, demonstrates that there is nothing to hide and that no one is putting anything over on anyone, begets confidence, and generates more and more trust. Closed secrecy has exactly the opposite effect: it suggests much to be hidden and it breeds suspicion; it goes with cunning manipulation and unsavory dealings; and it spreads a groundwork of mistrust which feeds upon itself and in which confidence and honesty cannot flourish.

Unfortunately, secrecy as between employer and employed is an outstanding characteristic of management in most democratic industrial nations.[1] This attitude of secrecy increases with increase in the size of the enterprise and with increase in the organization of employees into trade unions and staff associations. With the increase in the scale of organization there is an increased distancing between top management and the rest of the employees, and a growing sense of anonymity as they deal with each other through employee representatives.

Part of the reason for this secrecy is the widespread outlook that it is "management's job to manage and the employees' job to do the work they are employed to do." This outlook is as common in governmental employment as it is in private enterprise. In private enterprise the argument is that the directors and top management are acting on behalf of the owners, and it is therefore their prerogative to set policy and to manage the enterprise in line with the best interests of the owners. In government departments the attitude is the same, except that the rationale is the prerogative, and indeed the democratic duty, to act on

---

[1] The outstanding exceptions are, of course, Japan and West Germany. In both these countries, openness of management is widely regarded as having made a substantial contribution to economic success. In West Germany this effect is achieved through the established system of Works Councils, reinforced more recently by co-determination. In Japan, it is a result of the mutual respect of employers and employees which is deeply embedded in Japanese culture itself, and which is reflected in the actively operating assumption that all employees have a contribution to make in the development and introduction of new technology and procedures.

behalf of the electorate. In both cases employees are expected to fall into line.

The trouble with these notions about management prerogatives, and the accompanying feelings of top management's entitlement to keep their plans to themselves until they are ready to implement them, is that the work and career opportunities of the employees are at stake in whatever policies are being decided. It can be predicted that over the years employees will become increasingly restive at having foisted on them policies which affect their lives so deeply, without their having the chance to take part in formulating those policies. It has already led to legislation in many European countries to try to give employees a bigger say, but the steps taken there are inadequate. And in the United States the signs point toward growing employee unease which will lead in due course to the same questioning as has already occurred in Europe.

Here is a situation that is periodically disruptive and carries the potential for creating deep social schisms. It raises fundamental questions about the rights of employer and employees in relation to each other. Many experiments have been carried out in cooperative ownership, workers' control, worker directors, participative management, and in the abolition under socialism of private ownership itself. But none of these problems disappears or changes in any fundamental respect with change in type of ownership, despite Marxist theory, or theories of copartnership or cooperative ownership, or any other type of political theory. There may be initial honeymoon periods after revolutionary political changes or radical changes in employment organization, during which employment problems seem to be alleviated. But the same problems can be counted on to recur once the new political arrangements have settled down. Let us consider why they do, and what needs to be done to overcome them.

Ownership and Employment
The prime fact that must be recognized is that there are many different types of employer and employing associations but only one type of employment system. Consider the following list of institutions: private industrial and commercial companies; nationalized industrial and commercial companies; partnerships; democratic governments; socialist governments; communist governments; central governments; regional governments; state and provincial governments; county, city, and other types of local government; cooperative societies, self-employed entrepreneurs; universities; churches; voluntary societies; hospitals; private schools; registered clubs; trade unions; public authorities. Although they are all institutions which have been set up in order to get various kinds

of work done, they are nevertheless vastly different from one another in organizational structure. But there is one important respect in which they are all the same.

The similarity between these diverse institutions is that in order to get their work done they employ people on open-ended employment contract. And they all do so in the same way. Their governing body (whether a board of directors, a cabinet or council minister, a central executive committee, an appointed public commission or authority) appoints a chief executive officer (CEO), or perhaps several CEOs if there are several subsidiaries. The CEOs may have some such title as managing director, or general manager, or chief administrative officer, but the role is the same: it is to establish and manage an employment hierarchy to work to pursue the operating objectives of the enterprise.

As I have shown in Chapter 3, the employment hierarchies that are established are identical with one another in organizational structure and functioning;[2] that is to say, they are identical with one another in depth; and they display the same problems regardless of who or what the employing agency is.

The force of this finding about the universality of the structure and functioning of employment hierarchies is that the grave problems associated with the employment sector of employment societies are unlikely to be made to disappear by changing the character of the employing system. To be specific, a change to cooperative ownership as in the Mondragon development, or to state corporatism as under communism, or to workers' control as in Yugoslavia, or to cooperative communities as in the Israeli kibbutzim, will not solve the crises encountered in employment systems under capitalism.[3]

Regardless of the type of political control under which employment systems exist, employers still have to come to grips with employees. The organization of the work and the ensuing differential payment still

---

[2] In order to make myself absolutely clear on this point, I would draw attention to the fact that the employment hierarchies of universities and churches are the administrative departments and not the tenured academic staff or the clergy. University tenured academic staff and clergy are stipendiary members of the employing body, and it creates confusion to regard them, as tends so often to happen today, as salaried employees. Doctors treating patients also require to be established outside the employment hierarchies, but nurses and other professionals can readily be employed within them. A fuller treatment of these issues will be found in Elliott Jaques, (1976), *A General Theory of Bureaucracy;* and E. Jaques (Ed.), (1978), *Health Services.* London, and Exeter, New Hampshire: Heinemann Educational Books Ltd.

[3] This view is strongly underlined by the recent development of Solidarity in Poland and the demands of these union members for greater participation in policy-making in the state enterprises in which they are all employed.

have to be agreed upon. Who has the right to change the objectives or the work of the enterprise, to close down one office or factory or to open others, still has to be decided. Who should appoint the CEOs, who should be able to remove them, who should appraise the performance of others, who should decide who gets promoted, are all issues which go with employment hierarchies per se. What should be the rights of employees with respect to policy-making is an issue for any enterprise which employs people.

A free and just society must allow for a multiplicity of patterns of employing enterprise. But at the same time it must ensure that the employment systems established by those enterprises conform to a few basic requirements, including adhering to the equitable differential payment scale and the work-strata and grading system which have already been described. It must also ensure that open management becomes the order of the day, with adequate opportunity for employee participation.

Employee Participation

Given effective management at the top, a sound organizational and managerial structure throughout, abundant employment opportunity, equitable differential payment, and equality of opportunity including opportunities to start new enterprises, there yet remains the question of how to provide for employee participation in policy-making. This question is not just an industrial relations question to be left to the industrial relations staff in each enterprise to settle. That would be to impose a paralyzing limitation upon a matter of most profound political significance for a free employment society. It must be dealt with politically as the political problem that it is. For there are those who argue that so long as employees are well paid and well treated, to go any further in allowing for participation is to undermine management's prerogatives and its right to manage, and to encourage socialism. This argument is countered by the view that for employees to take part in policy-making is tacitly to uphold management and the existing political economic system whatever it might be, and to weaken employee independence of action.

Both these attitudes fail to take into account the realities of the power relationship in employment. Much of the bitterness in working life today arises from the growth of large-scale enterprises whose employees possess the franchise as citizens yet are dispossessed in their place of work. It is the present-day version of the constitutional crises which led to the steady extension of the franchise in the nineteenth century, ending with universal suffrage: the grand principle was no legislation without representation. Now the absence of the constitutional right to involvement in determining the policies which affect people at work is a living daily contradiction of their political freedom as citizens.

What is required—and in all public and social services as much as in industry—is not, for example, a token representation of employees on boards of directors, but a vigorous system of participation in each enterprise, achieving consensus on policy changes. It is this participation in policy-making which would extend the franchise for all who work for their living in employment systems. Industrial relations have moved into the position of one of the top social and political problems. The full creative energies of men and women will not be released until effective institutions to provide real participation are deeply rooted and widely understood.

Our work is of enormous psychological as well as economic importance to all of us. If we have no constitutional right to take part in determining the long- and short-term policies which have such a bearing on our work and careers, we are resentful, hostile, and suspicious—all readily predictable reactions of sound and sensible human beings feeling imposed upon by forces outside their control. Suspicion starts the process of alienation from work and withdrawal from reasoned argument; if things go wrong, even with well-intentioned management, withdrawal increases in the form of low motivation in work, or absenteeism. Finally, in the event of strong disagreements, collective withdrawal occurs, leaving management in an impotent position and reasoned debate difficult to reestablish.

Bitterness and resentment are probably more acute in Britain than in most other industrialized democratic nations. This state of affairs is not a reflection of British temperament. It arises because Britain was the first to industrialize, and the first and only country so far to reach the point where over 90 percent of its citizens who can earn a living do so in employment for a wage or salary; and over 11 million of the 23 million employed are collectively organized in trade unions.

It is for this reason of the scale and age of its industrialization that Britain is experiencing particularly difficult problems of industrial relations. Other industrial nations will encounter similar difficulties in the coming years, and would be well advised to learn from the unfortunate British experience. It is because of their seeming intractability that the problems of industrial relations—not only in industry but in the public and social services as well—move into a position of such importance for the survival of efficient and prosperous industrial communities, with humanity, democratic cohesion, and justice. Investment, production, exporting, imaginative new products, are all of great importance. But effort in these directions is increasingly thwarted because of nascent industrial tension and unrest.

Greater opportunity for open and constitutionally established rights must be provided. Employees must be given the opportunity to express their desires through constitutional channels of participation. Those channels do not exist. Until they do there is no outlet other than for varying degrees of noncooperation or disruption. By contrast, in the presence of constitutional channels radical thinking can become a lively stimulus to effective change.

Consultation and Participation

A number of processes, commonly referred to as consultation, must be sharply distinguished from constitutional participation as we shall define it here.

First there is the normal everyday consultation between a manager and his immediate subordinates—briefing groups, as they are often called. Such consultation, in which a manager keeps his subordinates informed and seeks their views and advice, is a fundamental requirement of effective manager−subordinate relationships. There is a regressive trend in some enterprises to refer to this ordinary activity of any good manager by the title of "participative management" and, because they believe that this is what participation is about, to think no further.

Second, there is the process whereby a manager will consult with elected representatives—for general discussion, usually excluding what are termed "negotiation issues" (that is to say, payment and conditions). In this process the manager appears to be free to take his own decisions after consultation. What is less commonly noted is that the representatives and their constituents, if dissatisfied, are also free to take the matter further, the mechanism being to issue threats or actually to exercise power by withdrawal in one form or another.

A manager, therefore, is not really free to make his own decisions after consultation, even though he may often sincerely believe that he is. If differences of aspiration are small or the issues trivial, the manager may get away with it. But where interests really diverge, a manager's decision to proceed without agreement appears to representatives as lacking in integrity. It makes them ask, "Why consult with us if you intend to proceed anyway?"

This sort of consultation, well-intentioned as it may be, breeds feelings of cynicism and distrust. As a reaction to this felt authoritarianism on the part of managers, the thoughts of the work force turn to consideration of the need to use its power to withdraw. The workers can institute a slowdown or a complete work stoppage. Morale suffers and active cooperation is at a discount.

If active use of power to disrupt the enterprise is threatened, then win-or-lose attitudes emerge which for a time will inhibit the ability of all parties to the conflict to debate it rationally; that is to say, such attitudes will inhibit the essential prelude to effective agreement.

In short, consultation procedures of this kind—while undoubtedly well-intentioned—are nevertheless in the final analysis built upon the very uncertain foundation of the power of withdrawal from reasoned argument and then from work itself. Resentment, touchiness, unease, are never far away—these are the feelings which breed distrust, make for unreasoned resistance to necessary change, and lead to explosive reactions to stress.

Managers and subordinates alike try to maintain the surface appearance of goodwill and reasonableness. But these attitudes do not strike deeply. Underneath there is little room for patient and rational work. There are too many unanswered questions surrounding the issue of "What if we—or they—do not agree?" The answer—either swallow it or fight—does not make for long-term progress in sound working relations.

Policy Decision-Making by Consensus

There are a number of fundamental conditions which must be established for policy-making participation. In the first place there must be provision for policy-negotiating bodies on each and every geographical site or complex of connected sites or departments on which there are more than 300 to 350 people employed (it is above this number that mutual recognition among employees is lost and anonymity sets in). Many enterprises would require several such bodies, and some would have a substantial number.

These negotiating bodies would determine all policies for the site they covered, within the constraints of such external policies as the law, national agreements between employers and trade unions, and agreements arrived at in the enterprise as a whole. They would have to be composed of the most senior executive on the site meeting with representatives of all employees. Not only manual workers but also managers, office staff, technicians, professionals, must be able to have representation in the policy-making processes. If these groups are unionized they will be represented by their own elected union representatives. If some are not, then mixed union–nonunion representation is called for. Each significant power group on site must be entitled to at least one seat at the negotiating table. By a significant power group is meant any organized group of employees which if it went out on strike could close the site down. That is the reality of the coercive power which must be contained within constitutional procedures.

Decisions must be by all-round consent expressed in a unanimous vote, that is to say, decisions must never be imposed by outvoting a protesting power group. This unanimity, or veto, voting is fundamental: the status quo obtains until change has been agreed on by representatives of all significant power groups, including management. To be absolutely specific: management would not impose unacceptable change upon employees; nor employee power groups upon management; nor—and this point warrants reflection—employee power groups upon one another.

The basic concept here is that no significant power group shall be coercively overridden by the imposition of a change to which it is determinedly opposed. The reality of power in these circumstances is the precipitation of industrial action, perhaps short of a strike at first but by a strike in the end. What people fail to see is that, once the strike has occurred, all-round agreement must certainly then be discovered by some means before work can be resumed.

The process of constitutional participation described has the effect of absorbing the physical conflict into due constitutional process around the conference table while work goes on. That is what due process is about. And paradoxically, far from slowing the process of decision-making and preventing change, the process described does just the opposite, as experience has shown: decisions are not only reached more quickly, but they are better, more carefully thought out and less patched up to reach desperate last-minute compromise.

The reason for these apparently paradoxical outcomes is not far to seek. They arise because once coercive imposition has been constitutionally debarred, it becomes possible for everyone to listen to other arguments and to give consideration to them; and it becomes essential to present rational arguments not just on a personal basis but on behalf of a real constituent power group made up of employees in the enterprise. The fact that sound constitutional arrangements give the greatest chance for rational argument and debate to take place (even though they cannot guarantee it) is one of their most constructive features.

It is the opposite arrangement—fragmented negotiations even if combined with consultation—which is destructive of sound decision-making. Fear of coercive imposition leads to suspicion, uncertainty, and to everyone's "playing it too close to the chest." Boards of directors and executives are unwilling to be too bold for fear of setting precedents that will be regretted. In such influences are the real sources of indecisiveness, unnecessary delay, and stagnation.

The unanimous decisions of these participative negotiating bodies have to be binding upon all the members represented, including the board of directors or the authority. Equally, where trade unions are represented by their shop stewards, the unions have to be willing to be committed. It is therefore necessary for there to be a wide circulation of agenda and minutes, not only within the enterprise but also to the local trade union offices so that no agreements can be made which are unacceptable within the unions.

The process described will be seen to be precisely the opposite of the common pattern of fragmented negotiation in which each power group negotiates separately and confidentially with top management. The result of such fragmented negotiation is the familiar leapfrogging, together with an avoidance of face-to-face debate among the negotiating groups: thorough-going consensus will not be achieved by those means.

Government employees would not of course take part in negotiations dealing with national or civil service legislation. Everyone must work within the law—including employee representatives in whatever enterprise—public or private—they may be employed. But within the law there is great scope for discussion and negotiation on all the varied means of implementing legislated enactments, and on work conditions and career progress opportunities.

Apart from acts and regulations agreed to by legislative bodies it is improper for a central government simply to impose its will on public and civil service employees. The decisions which the government makes in the course of implementing legislation must be subject to participation by employee representatives just as are the policies of the executive board of an enterprise. Apart from policies democratically agreed to in local authority debates, it is likewise improper for those authorities to impose their will on their own employees. The principles of participation must apply.

For a government representing all the people to reject employee participation in the name of the people would be to turn the democratic community into an autocratic management seeking unquestioning obedience to its management decisions from its public servants.

The lack of a constitutional right of staff and workers to take part in making the policies of employing institutions remains a central defect in the growth of political democracy in Western societies. Those democratic nations which can overcome this defect will—like Japan and West Germany which have gone a long way in this direction—have added a further dimension and further strength to the democratic way, and will have strengthened themselves politically and economically.

Given the development of full-scale employee participation of the kind described, even the question of possible layoffs within an enterprise—usually the source of intense acrimony and not infrequent employee sit-ins—can be handled constructively. The reasons can be put on the table and rationally debated, and, if accepted, the best way of handling the situation in terms of individuals can be considered. It is the combination of employee participation, with the assurance of abundant employment in the community and pay equity, which is the best guarantee of sound working relationships within employment systems.

CHAPTER 11

Equality of Opportunity

Political economy starts with human needs and with our absolute entitlement to work to satisfy those needs. There can be no temporizing with this condition, no allowing anyone to deteriorate on an unemployment slag heap; nor, as has been shown, is there any need to do so, as long as wage and salary differential equity can be assured.

Equity in wage and salary distribution can be assured by the introduction of the differential concertina and the elimination of the need for a labor market. It substitutes a democratic political process for a destructively coercive one. And, as we have seen, the conception of a labor market is in any case a fallacious idea—a powerful idea but fallacious nonetheless.

In short, in the argument I have pursued, the freely competitive commodity market has been preserved; the labor market has been removed; abundant employment and pay equity have been established; and economics becomes that much more human in the process.

In this last chapter I shall explore the implication of these conditions for one of the major political problems of our time: that of equality of opportunity—its meaning, and how to get closer to achieving it. It is the question of how to make possible a society in which all individuals, regardless of race, sex, class, color, religion, age, or family background, can have the opportunity to achieve the relative socioeconomic status to which they are entitled by their own efforts.

There will, of course, always be two limitations preventing absolute equality of opportunity: constitutional endowment of the individual; and family upbringing. Those limitations are facts of life's chances. But the question arises as to whether a third limitation should be allowed, namely, whether any individuals should be able to pick up higher socioeconomic status than they could achieve by their own capabilities, merely by means of the inheritance of wealth and economic position. In a society in which everyone is assured of the opportunity to enjoy abundant employment and equity pay, or competitive entrepreneurial opportunity, from the beginning of one's working career, any substantial additional inherited economic power could only precipitate the inheritors into relative positions beyond their capabilities—producing social disequilibrium and pushing the individual into a false and potentially demoralizing position.

Lastly, there remains the question of just how much people should work. If there can be as much work for everyone as we decide to have, how much work is enough? That will be a difficult question for any abundant employment society to decide. It will be a critical question in establishing what might be a good society.

Equality of Opportunity and Egalitarianism
There is no way, even if anyone wished to do so, in which people can be made equal, or in which they can live under egalitarian conditions in which all have equal socioeconomic status. In the first place, individuals will differ from one another in outlook and capability because they have different constitutional endowments and different childhood experiences. In the second place, even if egalitarian conditions were somehow arranged, there is no way of preventing different individuals making more or less use of the opportunities available—unless everyone is forced into a social and psychological straitjacket.

In referring to differences in endowment, I want to make it unequivocally clear that I am referring to differences between individuals and not to the possibility of racial differences. My concern is with how to achieve equality of opportunity for all individuals as individuals, and with the total elimination of the use of any social or political groupings as a reason either for limiting or for enhancing the status of anyone who happens to be a member of such groupings.

That individuals differ in constitutional endowment there can be no doubt: in emotional makeup; in level of capability and of potential capability; in particular types of skill and talent; in intensity of drive. These qualities may be influenced to greater or lesser extent by upbringing and education. But it is not true that social and educational deprivation necessarily prevents an individual's potential level of capability from maturing. No more is it true that educational and social advantages necessarily lead to full and rounded individual development.

What can be affected by social and educational deprivation are the opportunities which individuals may have to learn the necessary skills and knowledge to allow them to use their capabilities to the full at any given time. Such shortcomings can be overcome given sufficient freedom of occupational opportunity and related training.

No societies, then, can guarantee that all individuals will have either the same potential capability or exactly the same start. What they can do is to ensure that everyone will have the opportunity to find a full outlet for their capabilities in education and in work. The potential consequences for the development of society are incalculable.

Equality of opportunity under the conditions described vitiates any argument for egalitarianism. To try to make everyone the same is to deny the reality of individual differences, and to lose the solid freedoms that come with constructive entrepreneurial competition. To the extent that greater equality seems desirable to the people of a given nation, that can be provided by compressing the differential concertina. Even the compression of differentials, however, still leaves everyone free to enjoy their own preferences in life, and is not a compression into one uniform mode; and it would leave individual entrepreneurs free to gain their own relative positions within the economy. Equality of opportunity is a proper political economic goal; egalitarianism is not. Equality of opportunity leaves individuals free to sort themselves out relative to one another; egalitarianism forces them into a common mold and could be achieved only by a totally suppressive autocratic fiat.

Consequences of a Free Enterprise, Fair Employment Policy

A free enterprise, fair employment policy can transform industrial society as we know it. There are a number of substantial positive effects that would be stirred by unstinted encouragement of free enterprise combined with the assured availability of abundance of employment regardless of the numbers of people seeking employment, and with the fact that wage and salary equity was not only achieved but could be seen to be achieved because of the open democratic process by which it was determined.

One effect would be a complete transformation of the nature of the relationship between employer and employee, both in private entrepreneurial employment and in governmental public and social services employment. The day-to-day hacking at each other over pay and differential pay is eliminated. Effectiveness in terms of profitability and of cost reduction is no longer achievable by skill in coercive manipulation in pay bargaining. That pernicious practice goes. What is left is the opportunity for employers to organize and to arrange for the management of the work of the enterprise as effectively as they are able, paying the going wages and salaries; and the opportunity for employees to enjoy the differential incomes that go with giving a fair day's work at their level of capability.

In these circumstances, employers and employees both have an interest in the success of the enterprise, whether private or public. Private enterprise employers are concerned about profit and loss and the continuity of the business. Public sector employers (governing bodies on behalf of the public) are concerned about political success and survival. Employees, in both private and public sectors, are concerned about continuity of employment and career opportunity at equitable rates. Each is necessary to the other. No one will be motivated by the system into exploiting anyone else.

The effects of such arrangements upon individuals are likely to be very great. There is a potential reserve of goodwill in people which has not been tapped by socioeconomic arrangements so far, other than in times of war. This goodwill is shown in the norms of felt-fair pay which lie buried under the greed and ill-will whose expression is not only encouraged but actively demanded by the coercive and combative arrangements which have always obtained.

Once we can rely upon our constitutionally agreed procedures to produce equitable arrangements, we will place great value upon those procedures. Once abundant employment is assured, we will value that employment. Moreover, as citizens of a free enterprise, fair employment nation we will be able to trust one another, regardless of whether we are individual or corporate entrepreneurs, or managers or ordinary employees. We will be able to trust our society, instead of being alienated from it. We will be able to work for the common welfare— because we will be able to share fairly in its prosperity and can know that adversity too will be fairly distributed.

Inheritance and the Family

The possibility of true equality of political and economic opportunity raises, however, one of the great emotional problems in an employment society: what will happen to inheritance? It is a problem in which the interests of society, the interests of the family, and the interests of the individual not only meet but clash head-on.

The question of inheritance takes on a particular quality in democratic employment societies. That quality is produced by the apparently irresolvable conflict between, on the one hand, the rightful aspiration of every individual to have an economic start and continuing opportunity that is equal to anyone else's, regardless of family; while, on the other hand and at the same time, families and their individual members feel it to be only fit and proper to take special care of their own kind and to hand on from generation to generation any wealth accumulated by the family. Should the members of wealthy families have a decided advantage over the members of less prosperous families? Can this state of affairs ever be fair and just, either for the inheritors or for society?

At face value a society which succeeds in giving equality of economic opportunity to its citizens must also reduce the degree of special advantage provided by families to their own members; and they must reduce it to the point where family background cannot become a force which can subvert equality of economic opportunity. That would be to place the family in an invidious position in a free and just society, to turn the family into a socially disruptive force.

I have purposely formulated this last principle in terms of reducing the degree of special advantage and not in terms of eliminating it. For families will have profound effects for better or for worse upon their members: upon emotional stability and intellectual aspirations; upon values; upon knowledge and skills, including social skills; upon confidence and ambition; upon relations to school and learning and work; and upon nearly everything to do with people's socialization and emotional makeup and outlook, except for level of capability.

In these respects people will inevitably enter into political and economic life with different backgrounds and different outlooks and different degrees of preparation and ability to take advantage of socioeconomic opportunities. No society can run a uniform steamroller over social life; nor should it try to. Individual differences lie at the heart of a creative and adaptive society, and are to be encouraged and nurtured.

Recognizing that people at all socioeconomic levels will inevitably benefit or be handicapped to markedly different degrees by the quality of their family background, should families, in addition to those qualitative differences, be entitled to confer differential economic privileges, in the form of hard cash, by transferring wealth to one another, whether by gift or inheritance? That is a question which calls for sober and dispassionate consideration.

Given the equality of opportunity that would be conferred by a free enterprise, fair employment society, socioeconomic status gained by individuals could be gained by their own efforts. There would certainly be a differential status structure expressing differentials in individual capability. But that structure would change from generation to generation in response to the differential distribution of levels of capability in the individual members of each new generation.

The question then is whether inheritance should be allowed to distort the natural distribution of socioeconomic status. I would think not. Where there is true equality of opportunity for individuals, excessive income inheritance puts those who receive it into socioeconomic positions beyond their levels of capability. Such outcomes are false. They generate the false values that accompany living beyond what people are able to gain by their own efforts and abilities. The realistic expression of social esteem and prestige, as well as the proper earning of socioeconomic power, is at stake. Such esteem and prestige should reflect the ability of the person and not of earlier generations.

In principle, then, inheritance rights should be kept to a level that would not substantially distort the recipient's socioeconomic position in society. Such rights would be much less than holds currently in the democratic industrial societies. They could include such special provisions as allowing the inheritance of small family farm holdings, or the retention on leasehold of family homes and material possessions. At the same time, the withdrawal of opportunity to pass large fortunes from generation to generation could increase the investment funds in circulation—both for new businesses and for cultural, scholarly, and charitable endowment—by encouraging the economically successful individuals to disburse their fortunes in their own way rather than having them absorbed by taxation.

Work and Leisure

There is, finally, one other question which must at least be mentioned, even though it cannot be analyzed in detail, for it may seem that an inordinate emphasis has been placed upon work, especially employment work. The question is how essential is it for people to work for a living? It is currently common practice to try to reduce the length of the workweek in order to spread the available employment more widely. It is even a widely-held idea that, as technology develops, some people might not work for the whole of their lives and would have to be taught the effective use of leisure! Would it be possible to live a life of full-time leisure on social welfare payments? Or on a ten- or twenty-hour workweek? Is there a minimum required amount of work for equality of opportunity? What would a minimum workweek be if we were free to choose? Is there a difference psychologically between work and leisure?

These questions become particularly urgent if it is the case that any nation can have all the work it decides to have, for that leaves the question of what constitutes a reasonable workweek. There need be no question of reducing the workweek in order to spread available work more evenly. The reason for fixing a particular workweek would be to balance a desired GNP against the amount of time people wanted to spend working.

It is my long-held view that a proper amount of economic work is absolutely essential for mankind. I wrote, for example, and still hold that working for a living is one of the basic activities in the life of a man or woman. By forcing them to come to grips with their environment, with their livelihood at stake, it confronts them with the actuality of their personal capacity—to exercise judgment, to carry responsibility, to achieve concrete and specific results. It gives them a continuous account of the correspondence between outside reality and their inner perception of that reality, as well as an account of the accuracy of their appraisal and evaluation of themselves (even though they may not always desire to observe the account). And more, in the quality of enthusiasm or apathy which they bring to their work, they are faced with the state of the balance between the forces of life and the forces of death within them. In short, a man's or a woman's work does not satisfy their material needs alone. In a very deep sense, it gives them a measure of their worth and their sanity.[1]

In short, economic exchange work relates individuals to the realities of the world by making them do what is necessary to keep alive; and it relates individuals to one another and to their society in a material manner, in a manner related to the concreteness of goods and services available for use and summarized in a GNP and a standard of living.

How long a workweek is needed for the psychological well-being of the individual is, however, a question with no ready answer. The reduction from more than sixty hours a week to less than forty that has taken place in many industrial countries over the past hundred years does not contain the answer. For when our jobs match our capabilities we do not readily allow our actual hours of work to come down below forty. Self-employed shopowners or farmowners, for example, continue to work much longer hours; but of course they feel they are doing it for themselves, doing it to keep their businesses going. And they have under their own control the level at which they work, the level at which they run their businesses.

It is important, therefore, how we ask the question about the optimum workweek. It must be asked in terms of how long people need to have the opportunity to work at levels consistent with their capability on work which interests them. Given these conditions, my own estimate is that a period of 30 to 40 hours a week is likely to prove a minimum comfortable economic exchange work period for people. Individuals should be able to increase that amount of time; individual entrepreneurs, including husbands and wives working together, and employed managerial and specialist employees have never been limited to a fixed workweek and can readily extend their working time; manual workers and clerks can do so by arranged overtime work.

There are, of course, other kinds of work activity: in particular,

---

[1] Adapted from *Equitable Payment*, (1961), p. 3.

work in and with the family and voluntary work carried out for others without pay. Family work, especially for parents with growing children, may reduce for a time the time available for one or other or both parents to put into economic exchange work. But voluntary work should not be a substitute for economic exchange work.

My point is that neither family work nor voluntary work can really substitute for economic exchange work. They lack the valuation of a person's creativeness in terms of what others are willing to pay for it. That is why leisure, important in its own right, can in no way substitute for employment work or entrepreneurial work; it gives personal pleasure to the doer, and at its best contributes to personal reflection and personal insight, but it cannot substitute for the evaluation of oneself by others in economic terms.

Economic exchange work is one of the prime forces which hold industrial societies together; the continual sustaining of such a society requires equality of opportunity for its members to interact, in economic exchange and trade.

Coda

The free enterprise, fair employment industrial society which has been outlined has the following outstanding characteristics.

It is solidly based upon political equality—and sustains political equality by equality of economic opportunity for all individuals, regardless of social class, race, sex, color, religion, ethnic group, age, or family.

It recognizes individual differences and brings differentials in socioeconomic status into focus, into the center of our lives, and thus avoids the unreality of the economic egalitarianism which pervades some social thought.

Because it recognizes the importance of differentials it can provide for equity and justice in wage and salary differentials and remove human labor from the exploitative and coercive labor market.

It provides for continuous abundant employment, without wage—push and salary—push inflation and without any need for the totalitarian state corporate control exercised by many communist nations, with its Marxist rejection of freedom of enterprise and its inability to deal with differentials.

It brings a new and open relationship between employing enterprise and employees by removing from them the authority and the responsibility for settling differential pay, and thus removing the chronic disputation which saturates the relationship.

It changes the relationship between entrepreneurial status and prices and profits, on the one hand, and employee status and wages and salaries on the other hand, by opening the former completely to market forces, and by substituting politically determined equity in the marketplace for the latter.

By removing both the fear of unemployment and the organized coercion inherent in power bargaining over pay, it removes a prime source of crime and violence in society. And it brings a new openness and humanity to economic relationships and to political economy, enabling a nation to live within its means and in the process enhancing people's trust in their society, in themselves, and in one another.

Index

abstraction, level of, 79–85
alienation, 6, 20, 30, 49, 52, 74, 116–118, 126
arbitration, 99, 109
assessment of performance, 92, 105
ASTMS, 24

Bell, Daniel, 51
Billis, David, 78n, 80
bonus schemes, 15, 105
'brain drain', 99
Britain, 3, 4, 24–25, 51n, 73, 116; *see also* England

Cameron, Sheila, 73n
Canada, xvii, 99–100
capability, xiv, 52, 74n, 77–86, 92, 124, 125, 127, 129
capitalism, 19, 42, 59, 60, 114
career, 4, 48, 116
    development, xviii, 48, 63, 85, 92n, 105, 113, 126
civil service, 3, 120
coercive power bargaining, xvii, 9, 13, 15–26, 30, 43, 59, 65, 73, 94, 97, 99, 101, 104, 111, 118, 119, 123, 125, 126, 130
collective bargaining, 4, 15, 16–17, 21, 30, 61, 64; *see also* coercive power bargaining
communism, 114, 130; *see also* Marxism
comparability, xvi, 64, 68, 70, 100, 101
competition, xiii, 12, 32–33, 40–41, 97, 125
conciliation, 99, 109
consensus decision-making, 116, 118–121
consultation, 117–118
consumer, xi, xii, 12, 13, 29, 30–31, 38, 40–41, 42, 45, 60, 65, 106
contraction of business, 56, 111–112
cooperative
    communities, 114
    ownership, 113, 114

corporate
    executive vice president and time-span of discretion, 69–70
    group and level of abstraction, 84–85
    subsidiary and level of abstraction, 83–84
cost of living, 106–107

democracy, xi, 6, 19, 29, 30, 50, 52, 53, 59, 100–101, 104, 107, 112–113, 116, 120, 123, 125, 128
department manager
    and level of abstraction, 82
    and time-span of discretion, 69
Department of Employment, 73
deprivation, 40, 124
differential concertina, *see* wage and salary differential
disabled, 102
dividends, xiii, 102, 105
Drucker, Peter, 35n

Economist, 50n, 51n
egalitarianism, 97, 101, 124–125, 130
Eisenberg, P., 49n
"Empirical Examination of Elliott Jaques' Concept of Time-Span" (Goodman), 72n
employee
    -employer relationship, 111–113, 114, 115, 117–118, 121, 125, 130
    participation, xx, 97, 111–121
    protection, 4, 12, 47
    representatives, 108, 109, 112, 116, 117, 118, 120
    status, 36–37, 38, 41–42, 45, 48, 61, 62–63, 131
employment
    abundant, xiv–xvi, xix, 45–56, 60, 65, 75, 77, 92, 97, 98, 102, 104, 105, 106, 109, 110, 111, 112, 115, 121, 123, 125, 126, 130

133